Praise for *The Path to Revenue: Secrets of Successful Tech Leaders*

"*The Path to Revenue* is packed with wisdom gained from decades of work in Silicon Valley and twelve successful exits. This passionate book captures the importance of building a customer focus into your business, and gives eight practical strategies to do that. A must-read for any entrepreneur – sooner, rather than later."

–Geoff Moore, Author, *Crossing the Chasm* and *Zone to Win*

"GTM strategy is not easy but it's an essential part of every enterprise journey. *The Path to Revenue* is a must-read that offers eight strategies to keep the customer in mind when building a business and then going to market. C-suites and Boards need this perspective to thrive over the long haul."

–Ryan Floyd, VC and Founding Managing Director, Storm Ventures

"Theresa creates a blueprint for finding, evaluating and executing the creation of new markets, that drives new sales and enterprise valuations."

–Michael Sears, former Venture Capitalist and startup CEO

"This book underscores the central role of marketing in a business' success. A meaningful and digestible approach to scaling a company. Strongly recommend!"

–Steve Franzese, Independent Board Member and Former Fortune 500 CMO

"Marcroft lays out the tremendous benefits of forging a strong bond between sales and marketing – to focus on the customer. Theresa delivers insightful, collaborative success strategies in a clear, straightforward manner. Excellent!"

–Patricia Watkins, Author of *LAND and EXPAND–6 Simple Strategies to Grow Your Company's Top and Bottom Line*

"Intertwined sales and marketing teams are key to maintaining a customer-centric focus. Theresa shares a real world, pragmatic view of how sales and marketing professionals should work together to put their company on the path to revenue."

–Craig Lowder, Author of *Smooth Selling Forever*

THE PATH TO REVENUE

SECRETS OF SUCCESSFUL TECH LEADERS

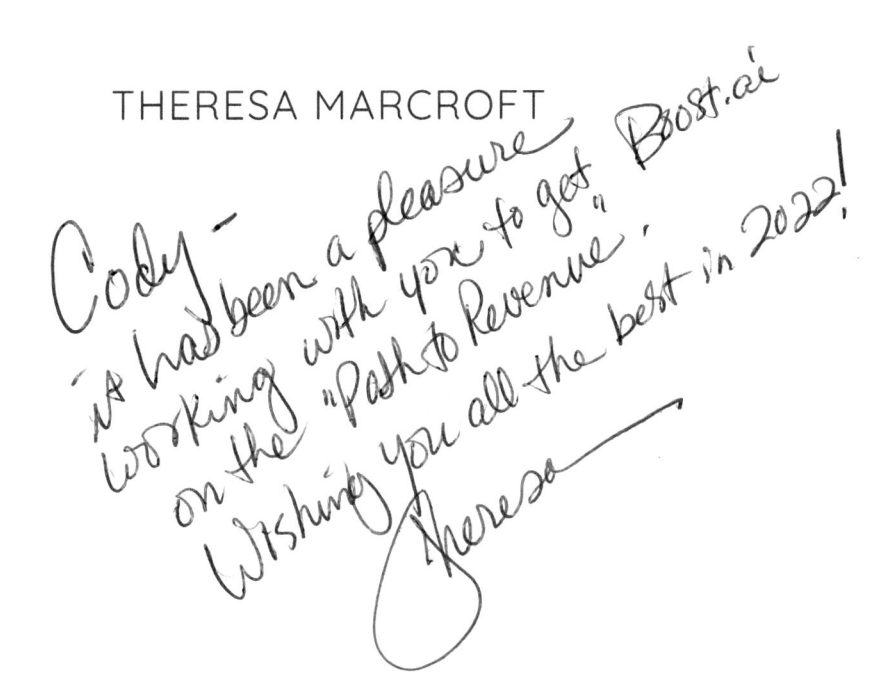

THERESA MARCROFT

GLOBAL PRESS OF SILICON VALLEY

Copyright © 2020 by Theresa Marcroft

All rights reserved.

Printed in the United States of America.

No part of this publication may be reproduced or distributed in any form or by any means without the prior permission of the publisher. Requests for permission should be directed to tmarcroft@market-savvy.com , or mailed to Permissions, Global Press of Silicon Valley, P.O. Box 28153, San Jose, CA 95129-8153

Neither the publisher nor the author is engaged in rendering legal, tax or other professional services through this book. The information is for business education purposes only. If expert assistance is required, the services of appropriate professionals should be sought. The publisher and the author shall have neither liability nor responsibility to any person or entity with respect to any loss or damage caused directly or indirectly by the information in this publication.

The stories in this book are based on truth, but when only a first name is used then names and some details have been changed to maintain privacy.

The Market Segment Characteristics™ matrix is a pending trademark of Theresa A. Marcroft.

The Buyer's Journey Matrix™ is a pending trademark of Theresa A. Marcroft.

The Customer Centric Approach to Market Strategy™ is a pending trademark of Theresa A. Marcroft.

Illustrations by geidesign.net

ISBN: 978-1-7357534-1-6 (Paperback)

ISBN: 978-1-7357534-0-9 (Mobi)

ISBN: 978-1-7357534-0-9 (ePub)

Library of Congress Control Number: 2020918250

GLOBAL PRESS OF SILICON VALLEY, P.O. Box 28153, San Jose, CA 95129-8153

www.market-savvy.com

To my Parents,
with Admiration, Love and Gratitude

CONTENTS

Preface: Why Follow Me?	9
Introduction	13
1. 90 Percent of Start-ups Fail: Here's Why	17
2. The Secret: Being "Customer-Centric"	31
3. Understanding Your Customers' Mindset	39
4. Communicating Value with Customer-Centric Messaging	53
5. Empowering Sales With Customer-Centric Content	67
6. Creating and Claiming your Market	85
7. Being Savvy about Channel Growth	99
8. Differentiate to Stand Out	113
9. Aligning Sales and Marketing	125
10. Defining Your Market Strategy	137
11. Tying it All Together: Be The One in Ten that Thrives!	151
12. Three Bonus Ideas	157
Parting Thoughts	165
Thank you!	169
Notes	171
About the Author	177
Acknowledgments	179

PREFACE: WHY FOLLOW ME?

Before we stroll towards the Path to Revenue, you should meet your tour guide. Navigating this path has been my life's work. I didn't always know the secrets of those successful tech leaders who beat the odds.

I discovered it the hard way.

The year was 2000. The place was Silicon Valley, California and my career was going gangbusters. After many years learning the ropes in a variety of corporate marketing roles for technology companies, I became VP of Worldwide Marketing for Cylink, a network security company. I was only working half time: twelve hours a day, seven days a week.

The role was global. Each quarter, I met with our people in Europe for two weeks, then visited their counterparts in Asia for another two weeks. After several seemingly endless transoceanic flights, I would split the remaining eight weeks of the quarter between the East and West Coasts. I wasn't home much. But I *loved* my job.

Despite the frequent international trips, my personal life was full. I couldn't wait to raise a family with my husband, a purchasing manager

PREFACE: WHY FOLLOW ME?

at a Fortune 100 company. Our gorgeous baby girl was healthy. Overall, attaining the desired balance was a delicate dance, but life was good.

Then the scariest event of my life blindsided me.

My marriage ended.

Suddenly, I had this new baby—godsend that she was—and we were splitting up and selling our house. I would become the sole breadwinner of my newly formed family of two, and I had to figure out how to make that work.

One thing was for sure: I couldn't keep up the status quo. The eighty-hour work weeks and frequent international travel were the first things to go. I needed to be in control of my schedule and my time. I wanted to be there to raise my daughter. It was clear: I had to reorganize my life. So, I thought about consulting.

What did I know about running a consulting business? Two sages in my life would shed light on 'making it' on my own, while two points of good fortune triggered my successful consulting career.

Back in the day, Regis McKenna Inc. was Silicon Valley's premier marketing and PR firm. Launching giants like Apple and Intel, no agency was better known for putting tech companies on the map. Being hired by Geoffrey Moore was a stroke of luck. He was Regis' business unit manager for enterprise software clients. He had not yet authored the highly successful book, *Crossing the Chasm: Marketing and Selling Disruptive Products to Mainstream Customers,* but we were living the experiences that would later add color to that book. Together we managed accounts with an emphasis on growing Regis' technology PR business.

During that time, Geoff taught me two valuable lessons:

- to understand and apply the "technology adoption life cycle curve" and
- how to win clients.

PREFACE: WHY FOLLOW ME?

Working at Regis was a training ground like no other. It was *the* premiere technology marketing firm for good reason. The people were brilliant, and the clients were the innovative powerhouses of Silicon Valley. I remain grateful to Geoff Moore and to Regis McKenna, Inc., for these valuable lessons, even though I didn't realize at the time how well they would serve me.

Even back then, there was a small voice in my subconscious hinting that I would be a consultant one day. I had a feeling that my independent streak would catch up with me.

The other gift of good fortune was fabulous parents.

When my sky was falling, I sought the counsel of my #1 hero, my Dad.

"So, you'll start your own business!" my Dad proclaimed. "It won't be easy, Hon, but you're a Marcroft, and you're quite persistent."

Persistent is his code-word for stubborn.

"You can do this." And then he gave me this advice: "Tell your clients the hard truth. You're not there to make friends; you're there to help them succeed and thrive. You've been training for years in your other tech marketing roles. Speak the truth with heart and you'll be doing them a great service."

Then he asked, "So, what is your big goal?"

"Dad, I have two goals. First, to be as great a parent to Sydney as you and Mom were to me. Second, to take on one client at a time, lead their marketing, and help make them successful. I'll dig in, roll up my sleeves, and devote myself to each company that I engage. With that focus, I believe I can eventually help about ten young Silicon Valley firms succeed."

Well, I'm here to say that my dear Dad was right: it was *not* easy! Fast forward through two decades of tech marketing. I worked with each client full-time, on contract, for six to twenty-four months. I've helped not ten but twelve different companies get onto the path to revenue.

PREFACE: WHY FOLLOW ME?

I went *all in* with each of those companies, working with them as their interim chief marketing officer—doing the CMO job on a consulting basis.

And here's the kicker. Not only did I always have a paycheck, working with my Silicon Valley clients blessed me with the ability to raise my daughter the way *I* wanted. I got to teach math weekly in her parent-participation school; I got to chaperone the fifth-grade science camp, the seventh-grade trip to Mexico, and the eighth-grade trip to DC. As our house was just a block from the high school, I got to provide the cookies and ice cream so that *my* home became the after-school gathering place.

Clients came to me as I needed them and money was never an issue. On average, I invested about eighteen months in each client. A few longer, a few shorter. I wrapped up all the loose ends at the completion of each engagement, often interviewing VP Marketing candidates for them and providing a smooth transition from my work to the "permanent" executive.

I won't claim that each client took my advice about *everything*, but they went with most of my recommendations.

I've learned a lot about leveraging the power of marketing to make companies successful. I saw many CEOs make decisions that led to the demise of their companies. I also witnessed several CEOs embrace tough decisions; strategic calls that turned out to be the most important choices they made to put their companies on the path to revenue.

With the benefit of hindsight and my firsthand experiences, we can apply those lessons to lead to *your* success.

This is my parting gift to the next generation of tech company leaders. I've distilled the knowledge I gained over twenty years of "interim VP marketing" consulting work into eight key concepts of customer-centric businesses. If you take this advice to heart, and put your customer at the center of your focus, your company *will be* on the path to revenue.

—*Theresa Marcroft*

INTRODUCTION

An entire career in Silicon Valley technology marketing has afforded me a unique vantage point. Not a striking view of the distant horizon—like the one you observe from atop the Eiffel Tower. If you want to your business to grow and succeed, my vantage point is far more helpful.

Through my technology marketing firm MarketSavvy, I've advised many public and private company CEOs on marketing strategy. My consulting career has thrived in Silicon Valley: I have guided three companies to successful IPOs, five to profitable acquisitions under favorable terms, and four companies now reach over $10 billion in annual revenues today.

That experience has been captured and condensed in this book, because I want to help you thrive. If you embrace the lessons ahead, your company will vastly improve its chances for success.

> *The principles in this book apply to any entrepreneurial organization; be it a young "startup", a small- to medium-sized company, or a Fortune 100 spinoff.*

INTRODUCTION

The concepts in this book have consistently helped many young companies go to market, avoid fatal mistakes, and find the path to sustainable revenue.

One thing is for sure; it's a *heck of a lot harder* to go from zero revenue to $1 million annually than it is to increase revenues by ten percent—by $50 million—if you are a $500 million company. Of course. It's harder for a car to go from zero to 60mph than it is to go from 60 to 70mph. The speeding car already has the momentum. The car that's just getting started has to overcome inertia, find a driver, chart a course, fill the tank, etc.

I've helped companies make that leap to sustainable revenue countless times.

I'm an insider who's seen some companies succeed and entirely too many fail.

Here's what failure looks like.

A CEO with a great idea for a new technology product assembles a small team. They work together closely, ten or twelve hours a day, for twelve or eighteen months. Maybe for two or three years.

All that time, they're individually and collectively investing their blood, sweat, and tears into their exciting venture. Each work day is long and packed, family time is minimal, and their social life takes a backseat like a tourist in an Uber.

The focus for one and all is on completing development. Finishing this product. When that's done, they'll have succeeded.

But they don't.

Nine times out of ten, ventures like that never become more sustainable than a surf shop in Alaska. I've observed this cycle firsthand, as it repeats itself. Over and over.

My career has been all about being customer focused. From my client work, I've identified the top eight strategies for implementing a customer-centric focus. These can make or break your company.

INTRODUCTION

In this book, I'll impart real life anecdotes from my decades of work with Silicon Valley companies. My motivation is to share these insights so that others can succeed.

These are my lessons learned.

I hope that the coming decade will see many more startups and small businesses transition successfully from superb idea to sustainable company. I want your company's journey to be smoother than most, and hope you will travel, and enjoy, the path to revenue.

All the stories in this book are true. They are actual case studies based on my memory of my work with clients. I have not mentioned client names for confidentiality and I've changed all individual names to protect privacy.

1

90 PERCENT OF START-UPS FAIL: HERE'S WHY

> This material focuses primarily on marketing, because that is where the leadership must come from."
>
> —Geoffrey A. Moore, *Crossing the Chasm: Marketing and Selling Disruptive Products to Mainstream Customers*[1]

Nine of every ten start-ups fail.

They go bankrupt. The owners throw in the towel. They cease to be.

The first time I heard that startling statistic, it was hard to wrap my brain around that. How could that happen?

But it's true. Nine of every ten companies don't make it beyond their first five years in business.

They never get to a revenue run rate that even comes close to covering their expenses. They don't successfully navigate the rocky path to a sustainable business, and, as a result, never get to enjoy the fruits of their labor.

Why is that?

It's because they are missing out on this secret: If you want to avoid being a mere statistic—drowning in a sea of failed companies and doomed startups—you must adopt a *customer-centric mindset.*

The Customer-Centric Mindset

The concept is simple but vital.

The customer mindset should influence (not dictate) all major decisions involved in starting and growing a business. Run your business with your customer in mind. Let your customers' preferences, expectations, and mindset influence all your key business decisions.

The customer mindset is a key reason Netflix' streaming option conquered Blockbuster's "pickup-and-return" model. It provided greater convenience to the customer. That same customer mindset played a role in the train replacing the horse as a daily mode of transportation, then the car replacing the train. They each made life more convenient for the customer.

However, this isn't as simple as creating a better product, and it involves so much more than marketing.

You must bake the customer mindset into the company, like chocolate chips in a cookie.

Adopting a customer-centric perspective will benefit your business at every turn. Running your business with your customer in mind will put you on the path to revenue.

And there is no better path.

Let's address one thing right up front: adopting a customer-centric mindset is the business of the *entire* company. *All* of your employees should think about the customer.

Limiting that responsibility to just the marketing and sales departments is like asking only one police precinct to worry about crime, rather than expecting this to be the focus of the entire police force. If the marketing and sales teams are the only people in the company thinking about the customer mindset, you're in a precarious position.

Often, it's the marketing leadership that reminds others of that. Given that responsibility, marketing is a key discipline that should be a top priority of your company.

Too often, I've met with CEOs who are unclear on what marketing brings to the business. As a result, it's often the last role hired in the C-Suite. One CEO I talked with boasted that he had grown revenues from X to Y without marketing. Then he confessed, "I'm not even sure what marketing would do for me."

Really?

This is like wondering what a co-pilot brings to the airplane.

Marketing charts the course from Point A to Point B, from a revenue level of X to Y. From one product to many. From one niche market to several vertical markets. From unknown brand to market leader.

The short answer is marketing will help you achieve your goal and realize your vision. You accomplish this by keeping the customer focus front and center. That's often the difference between success and failure.

To be clear: Having a customer-centric mindset does not mean customer *driven*. Don't allow your customers to "drive" your business, or customer requests to create your priorities. You don't need to add every feature they ask for or every bit of functionality on their wish list. (Saying "no" enables you to focus on your chosen market, satisfy those early customers and then move on to the next market niche.) There's a time and place for customer input to be thoughtfully considered as you define your roadmap.

Reacting to each customer demand is not what I'm advocating here.

Instead, a customer-centric mindset adopted throughout the organization means keeping the customer perspective in mind. How does a change you're considering impact the typical customer? How can you best serve all your customers? What trends are your customers living with and adapting to now? All of this goes into your customer-centric mindset and forms the backdrop to your decisions.

How We Think About Marketing

Here's a rather universal definition of marketing that shows traditional thinking:

> *Marketing is the process of* defining, declaring, and delivering *products and services that your customers want or need.*

The last word of this definition is the most important: *Customers.* The 90 percent of companies that fail in the first five years did not concentrate foremost on the customer.

For many companies, marketing is really just the 'communicating' part. They likely focused their efforts and marketing budget on pushing the message out over Twitter and Instagram. With all due respect for the power of social media, it's not enough. That one-way, short-lived communication it isn't the best onramp to the path to revenue.

A *customer-centric mindset* elevates your marketing effort to an entirely new level. Let's take another look at this definition of marketing, putting the emphasis on the *customer*...

> Marketing is the process of defining, declaring, and delivering products and *services* that your customers want or need.

Consider these points:

Define your product or service. Base the decisions about your product offering on customer need and refine them with customer input. Allow the market to influence your decisions about what to make ... in the big picture as well as the granular details.

You must gather customer feedback every step of the way. Career marketers cringe when they hear their CEO say, "Our customers don't know what they're talking about!" Customer feedback is vital. The larger question may be, "Is that company hearing what their customers are saying?"

Customer need and customer input are the yardsticks that guarantee there's a market for the product you're making.

Or not.

Declare your offering. Declaring, or communicating, is not only about persuading your customers to buy from you.

*Communication, by definition,
is a two-way exchange of information.*

It is how you articulate your competitive value, how you choose words that will resonate with your customer, and how you digest the feedback you get.

If you've completed this step well, if you've really been listening to your customers, both you and your target customer will be convinced that your product is a superior solution compared to competitive products.

Deliver, or make available. Delivering your product or service has to do with pricing, packaging, sales and distribution channels, special promotions—everything involved in making your product accessible and easy for your customer to buy. It also may mean making the product *itself* customer accessible; easy to use, intuitive, cool. You remove all obstacles to finding, buying, and using your product or service.

Customer-centric marketing begins with the very first steps you take in refining your idea and forming your business. It shapes your daily outlook more effectively than your breakfast of champions. The *customer-centric* outlook becomes the frame of reference for each decision you make.

You can firmly plant your feet on the path to revenue if you embrace customer-centric marketing as the secret to viability, sustainability, and growth.

It's your key to success.

Customer-centric marketing is the mindset that gives you a fighting chance. Deploying customer-centric marketing correctly will increase your odds of success exponentially.

Why not widen the goalposts before you kick?

When 90 Percent Of Start-ups Fail

So many entrepreneurs dream of being the next Steve Jobs.

If *only* we could be the next Apple. And why not? Many become entrepreneurs because they've developed a breakthrough technology. Something innovative. Something never before accomplished or offered.

Sad to say, many start-ups get the Wile E. Coyote treatment and are led off of a cliff by the very entrepreneur that gave them life. It's a heartbreaking truth that approximately 90 percent of Silicon Valley's technology companies fail in the first five years.

As Katie Benner put it in her New York Times article, "Silicon Valley is always eager to celebrate its success stories, but many tiny start-ups (that few ever hear about) form the tech industry's dysfunctional underbelly."[2]

According to New York data and research company CB Insights, 70 percent of upstart tech companies fail within about twenty months of initial financing. The failure rate is even worse for consumer hardware start-ups with 97 percent of seed crowdfunded companies failing.[3]

And when the company implodes, the *cost*—in venture capital, in everyone's time and energy, in missed market opportunities, in unproductive career detours—is nothing short of staggering. Not to mention the personal disappointment and heartbreak.

THE PATH TO REVENUE

All while social lives fizzle and family ties strain.

The backstory doesn't have to remain a mystery. Thanks to recent research, we can analyze the reasons most of these new companies go belly up like your childhood goldfish.

This insight, along with some practical tips and case studies, will improve your odds of getting on the path to sustainable revenue growth.

The Reasons So Many Start-ups Die

A 2019 survey conducted by research firm CB Insights lists the top ten reasons, based on their analysis of detailed post-mortems, for the failure of 101 start-ups[4]:

TOP 10 REASONS STARTUPS FAIL

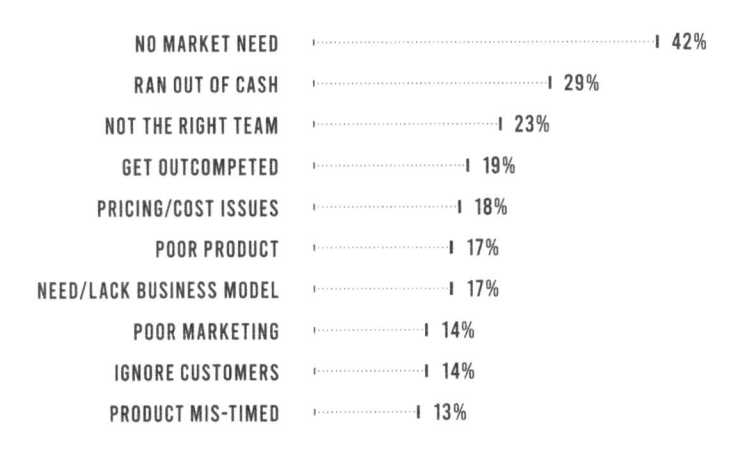

Reason	Percentage
NO MARKET NEED	42%
RAN OUT OF CASH	29%
NOT THE RIGHT TEAM	23%
GET OUTCOMPETED	19%
PRICING/COST ISSUES	18%
POOR PRODUCT	17%
NEED/LACK BUSINESS MODEL	17%
POOR MARKETING	14%
IGNORE CUSTOMERS	14%
PRODUCT MIS-TIMED	13%

RESEARCH BY CB INSIGHTS, 2019 — CBINSIGHTS.COM/RESEARCH/STARTUP-FAILURE-REASONS-TOP

CB Insights conducted a postmortem review and analysis of 101 failed startups. While there is rarely just one single reason for any startup's failure, CB Insights detected patterns in the stories. The chart above reveals the most common reasons start-ups fail.

#1: Market Need

The most often-cited reason is "no market need." There is a connection between adopting a customer-centric mindset and ensuring that there is an actual customer for the product. There's much more on that to come.

Sometimes a business can succeed without existing demand simply because it's quirky. An example of this is PotatoParcel.com, a direct-to-consumer business that allows people to mail potatoes with personalized messages written on them to someone else.

Yes, potatoes with writing on them.

You can do this anonymously, if you prefer.

The owners of Potato Parcel appeared on ABC's *Shark Tank*, made a deal with shark Kevin O'Leary, and it remains one of O'Leary's top five favorite investments. The business makes more than $25,000 profit each month.[5]

Silicon Valley start-up execs fail 90% of the time, while the Chief Potato Officer is living a good life.

That concept is laughably simplistic, yet profitable. It didn't fulfill a market void, but it was quirky enough to gain traction. The potatoes were novel and entertaining.

That's a rare exception.

The tech world, however, requires a consumer in need. A lot of them.

#2: Sufficient Cash

"Ran out of cash," the #2 reason cited, means that something *else* went wrong— the company misjudged demand or sales price. They underestimated the cost to make the solution or made an unwise choice of distribution strategy. The design was missing key features. Many things can delay revenues as cash reserves dwindle.

#3: The Right Team

"Not the right team," the #3 reason cited, seems like a cop-out for a few reasons. Executives in Silicon Valley are often not the best interviewers and have been known to hire for all the wrong reasons. They hire friends, in-laws, fellow alumni—not because they are qualified for the job at hand, just *because*. We can become much better at hiring well if we make it a priority.

#4: Competition

Another top reason (#4) that start-up companies die a painful death, according to CB Insights, is that they get out-competed. This is key.

If one of your competitors is doing a better job of meeting your customers' needs, it might be because you're not listening to your customers. The competition might be offering a product that suits your customer just fine, while your product or service is just not right for the user. Perhaps the competitor's delivery is superior, or their customer service is more user-friendly, or they have more desirable features.

#5: Pricing and Cost Issues

#6: Poor Product

Notice a Trend?

Upon closer examination, the real cause of death for most start-ups is either market-related or market*ing*-related, by an overwhelming majority.

Quickly avoiding that fate, and successfully traveling the path to revenue, is the challenge at hand.

Technology In Search Of A Market

The number one reason small companies fail is "No market need." Despite their good intention, the founders of almost half of the startups built a business around something for which there is no demand.

Novelty items like pet rocks, mood rings, and message-bearing potatoes aside, if there's no real need for the product or service they're making, the venture is doomed from the start. Yet, a surprising *42 percent* of young companies learn the hard way that there's not a significant market for the product they've created.

These companies are creating *a technology in search of* a market. This is the case with many start-ups—too many!

The engineers are proud of their technical accomplishments with all the functions and features ("speeds and feeds," as we say in Silicon Valley), but the practical application was just not in high demand.

The delay in getting that product in front of customers so that the engineers can add this extra feature is a kiss of death —especially when that added functionality was not deemed desirable or needed by the customer.

You're better off if you identify the market need first, confirm it by talking with actual customers, and then develop the technology to meet that need.

If that sounds obvious, here's an example. One technology start-up company I worked with wanted to sell a product to DIY homeowners, but it required customers to be computer-savvy. They had to figure out complex screens and even do a bit of coding. Even the handiest contractor-type DIY homeowners may not be super savvy with computers. And this was the target customer.

Ease of use can be a benefit, but if it's missing, it's an obstacle. Here, it was a deal-breaker.

It turns out there *was* a market need for this particular DIY product, with the features and functionality offered. But, since handy do-it-yourself guys were the target user, the product also had to be intuitive and easy to use. This product, however, required coding skills that the target customer did not possess, and didn't want to learn.

Success comes when people want to buy and use what you're offering, at the price you're asking, with the features they need that you have. Anything else will just not fly.

The "Build A Better Mousetrap" Myth

Many start-ups believe, "If we build it, they will come." They spend their time engineering the "best" product. They define "best" and then they refine it. And then they refine it some more.

They create version 1.0, then v2.0, then v2.1, then v2.1.2, adding feature after feature—ever increasing the coolness factor. They obsess over the technology itself rather than the (tech-based) *solution* they are providing for the customer.

The customer is—quite literally—an afterthought.

Their internal dialogue looks something like this: *"If we use a 'Six Sigma' approach, we could make it 10 percent faster! If we add another port.... If we increase functionality..... If we comply with this standard..... If we add these bells and whistles... If. If. If... then the world will be in awe. Our product will be a thing of beauty. Of course, it will sell."*

But it doesn't.

This mentality is literally *killing* companies. It's a fatal and presumptuous miscalculation to think that if you keep adding features to your product, it will soon be perfect.

Then, when it's perfect, you'll be the market leader. You'll take market share from the competition and customers will flock to you. It's a common misperception that the best product will win the day.

The best product does *not* always win the day.

Is Microsoft the best software on the market? Absolutely not. Does McDonalds offer the best cuisine? Stop laughing. Is Budweiser the best beer? Not even close. Is Domino's the best pizza? *No, no, no.* And yet these companies dominate their respective markets.

Microsoft dominated, bought, or crushed the competition in court.

Any company that had Microsoft as its principal competitor in the 1990–2010 timeframe is long gone. Microsoft is an undisputed market leader. But not because they had the best product.

McDonalds does not take first place in a taste test, in nutritional value, in breadth of menu, or even in convenience. Yet it's number one in fast food (and awkward clown mascots).

Bud Light became America's favorite beer in 1982 and remains the market leader today by a two-to-one margin.[6] There is no way you could convince me that Bud Light is the tastiest beer in America, but their brilliant marketing in Super Bowl ads proves they are king and it helps them stay there.

Dominos reinvented themselves in 2009. An employee video had forced a wake-up moment in which the company realized that both their image and their taste rankings were poor. They set out to correct both—with a passion. Improving ingredients, promoting their delivery vehicles, and encouraging online ordering paid off. By 2015, half their orders were placed online and half of those came via mobile.[7] Pizza scored higher on consumer tests. These factors accounted for a rise in market share from 9% in 2009 to 15% in 2016—the fastest growth rate among top chains.[8]

Which poses this question: What makes a company a market leader? The best product? No. The first product? No. The lowest price? No. It's not the best product that wins. It's not even the most customer-centric product that wins.

It's the companies with a *customer-centric focus* that win.

One In Ten Find The Path To Revenue

Hopefully, it's crystal clear by now that it's not the best mousetrap that wins. It's the company that best understands its customer. To be one of the 10% that survive and thrive, you *must* embrace the concept of customer-centric marketing.

THE PATH TO REVENUE

This book contains actual case studies— examples of customer-centric marketing put into action. Each of the coming chapters contains at least one "lesson learned" along with examples of a scenario that called for application of that lesson. When you apply these customer-centric marketing lessons, you can overcome the most common obstacles, confront the many pitfalls, and conquer the challenges to which most young companies succumb. You can win these battles. They *are* surmountable.

Only one in ten young companies can survive, thrive, and win because so few know the secrets of successful tech leaders who beat the odds.

The vast majority failed because they didn't create a product that fully met their customers' needs and wants. Their marketing wasn't customer-centric. Their *company* wasn't customer-centric.

But when they file for bankruptcy, at least we can mail them a "condolences potato."

Satisfying your customers is always paramount. The case study in the next chapter teaches another important lesson: even a desirable product requires precise marketing to avoid the graveyard of failure.

2

THE SECRET: BEING "CUSTOMER-CENTRIC"

The first Trader Joe's store opened in 1967 in Pasadena, California[1]. Trader Joe's got its start offering fresh local products and has thrived in the highly competitive supermarket industry ever since. Decade after decade, the number of store locations[2] quintupled and revenue shot through the roof.

What's behind their success?

Innovation. Trader Joe's (TJ's) is known for its innovations, such as paper bags with handles and the wine that earned the nickname "Two Buck Chuck" (if this existed while I was in college, I may have never graduated!). Granola was first in a long legacy of quirky private label products. For decades, the chain has rolled out on average ten new items each week, including chili jam, garlic herb pizza dough, and cookie butter, that have quickly become customer favorites. A customer's request resulted in selling bananas by the piece instead of by the pound, thus the advent of the 19-cent banana.

Customer Relations. Trader Joe's empowers their employees to build customer relationships, answering every question (employee product knowledge is a priority) and listening to comments and suggestions. In fact, Trader Joe's is known for their staff, called "crew members," and they expect them to deliver a customer experience that is warm, friendly, knowledgeable. The idea is that whenever someone walks out of a Trader Joe's store, they feel a little better than when they walked in. The staff learns how to do this at Trader Joe's University, TJU. Check out the "Inside Trader Joe's" podcast, "Why is Everyone So Nice?" (Season 3, Episode 14)[3]. It's all about what motivates the TJ crew members to treat customers so well.

Value. The core brand promise is value—quality products at appealing, everyday prices. To deliver that core promise, they leverage their investment in customer relationships to get feedback on each innovation. (You can return anything at TJ's without even bringing the receipt or the product with you: just tell the cashier and they'll subtract that amount from your bill.)

"If you have more money than brains, you should focus on outbound marketing. If you have more brains than money, you should focus on inbound marketing."
–Guy Kawasaki

Have you noticed that Trader Joe's doesn't advertise? There are no online ads. There are no in-store sales. No flyers in the Sunday newspaper. No loyalty discounts. Even the occasional radio ads focus more on the company and culture rather than the products[4].

Instead, they put most of their marketing dollars into product samples for customers.

Innovation. Value. Customer relations. Trader Joe's is a great example of what it means to be "customer-centric." They demonstrate customer focus in action.

A Note on Market Research

Imagine ...

Imagine that Trader Joe's, back in the early days, had done extensive market research to test their business plan. The project consisted of polls and surveys and ten kinds of questionnaires to determine if their idea would fly. They were thinking of creating a new kind of food store that would be smaller and offer one-tenth the number of products typically stocked by a traditional grocer. Customers could sample anything, any time with no obligation to buy the product, and enjoy a no-questions-asked return policy. The store would not hold promotional sales or offer coupons but would ensure a wide variety of vegan, kosher and gluten-free items. Plus there'd be lots of quirky products with unique flavor combinations. Packaging on all store brands would be environmentally friendly. On top of that, at each store the staff would sport Hawaiian shirts and the décor would feature plastic lobsters.

Sound like a winning combination?

Often—especially when you're offering something new or different—market research may not be helpful. There are two reasons for this. First, if you try, you can usually find a set of data to support *whatever* conclusion you want. Second, customers don't know whether they want that offering if it has not yet landed on their radar.

In the early days of concept testing, there's a *lot* to be said for going with your gut—especially if there's no market for the offering. If you reject the naysayers and move forward anyway, then you'll get the chance to create a new market, create "demand" and win over early customers. Then, you'll gather input from them. Observing, listening and acting on *that* is the key to improving your offering and growing your customer base.

No traditional market research professional would have predicted the opportunity for Trader Joe's.

That may be why Guy Kawasaki, in his book, Rules for Revolutionaries, says, "Nothing is more important than gathering information about your customers and your competition, so you should never leave it to the market research professionals.[5] They would not have asked the right questions or 'pressed the flesh'. They would have missed huge opportunities by asking, when they should be observing.

Instead, earn your early customers. Then watch and listen.

Creating Rabid Fans

Trader Joe's chief focus has always been the customer.

As a result, they are recognized for both innovation and record revenue per square foot. They are known for both low prices and personality. And for consistently outperforming the rest of the grocery industry.

Have a suggestion? It's welcomed with enthusiasm. Want a store in your town? Their website offers you a form to request one in your city. Gluten-free, kosher or vegan? They've got you covered. No gimmicks, no promotions, no coupons. Just everyday great value.

By 2020, TJ's had exploded from the original single store to over 500 locations, spread over forty-two states and Washington D.C.

People *love* their TJ's, as evidenced by their faithful customer base, which is often described as 'cult-like.'

My sister is looking for her retirement town, and she'll only consider cities with a TJ's. That customer loyalty is born from customer-centric companies, and Trader Joe's is a customer-centric organization if ever there was one.

All of that—value and low prices, unique products and innovation, personality and quirkiness—add up to one wildly successful example of the customer-centric mindset in action. CNBC reports that *Edge* by Ascential, a retail insights company, states that Trader Joe's enjoyed $13.7 Billion in revenue in 2019.[6]

The company's leadership likely enjoyed that meteoric rise to success. Which is my goal for your company too.

And you can do it.

The focus of this book is B2B. I chose to illustrate using Trader Joe's, a B2C example, because it's familiar and most people can relate.

The marketing principles in this book apply to both B2B, as well as the B2C sector, and are not just for startups. Any small company that is

THE PATH TO REVENUE

trying to grow and build a sustainable revenue stream will benefit from my experience.

As long as you don't lose focus on the single, most important aspect of your business.

The customer.

Eight Customer-Centric Strategies

Here's where we're headed in this book.

First, we looked at why so many startups fail (Chapter 1). In this chapter, we see the customer-centric mindset in action in the Trader Joe's story (Chapter 2). Now that we are clear on the importance of having a customer-centric mindset, we'll focus on *eight key strategies* to implement a customer-centric focus. These are eight ways to check—and ensure—that your organization is adopting a customer-centric approach to doing business.

Each of the following eight chapters includes the lesson learned, at least one case study from my consulting business, application tips and final thoughts.

Understand Your Customers' Mindset (Chapter 3).
Understanding the technology-adoption life cycle will shed light on various views on adoption of new technologies. Some people are early adopters and some are late adopters. How do you figure out which target market applies to your product? How do you understand the mindset of that target market? Chapter 3 discusses one of the smartest, savviest endeavors that any technology company can make. It also influences how you market to that group.

Customer-Centric Messaging Communicates Value (Chapter 4).
Value-based messaging is a rare thing of beauty here in Silicon Valley where tech-speak abounds. Quoting your product data sheet will not get you anywhere. Communicating the benefits you offer your customer does. Chapter 4 will provide a guide to describing your message succinctly.

Empowering Sales With Customer-Centric Content (Chapter 5).
The last decade has brought significant changes to traditional B2B sales. How do buyers of business products and services want to get their information? How do they want to make purchase decisions? Great content is the engine that powers great marketing. And making it available to the right people at the right time is key. In Chapter 5, I will analyze the importance of content marketing, how social media fits in, and a new strategy you must embrace.

Create And Claim Your Market Niche (Chapter 6).
Category creation is a powerful and often insightful growth strategy. However, many company leaders can find it intimidating. Is defining your own market niche actually the smartest approach? If you can pull it off, you can be king of your own (newly created) market. In Chapter 6, I will review the pros and cons of market creation and cite several examples from which we can learn.

Be Savvy About Channel Growth (Chapter 7).
If channel partners will give you access to customers you wouldn't otherwise sell to—such as internationally— then you might set up a channel program. There's a time and place to branch out beyond the US market, but it's not a revenue level or product type that makes you ready. In Chapter 7, I will give my best advice and several points to consider before adding indirect sales and/or moving overseas.

THE PATH TO REVENUE

Differentiate To Stand Out (Chapter 8).
Your differentiation must be intentional. It's about giving your customer a compelling reason to buy your product or service instead of that of your competitors. In Chapter 8, I will show you how your company can benefit by differentiating wisely, based on three variables.

Align Sales And Marketing (Chapter 9).
We are partners, not adversaries. Getting your company on the path to revenue focuses on one of the easiest problems to spot but hardest to fix because the issue stems from inside—the people, not the process. In Chapter 9, I will review some keys to ensuring sales and marketing alignment.

Define your Go-To-Market Strategy (Chapter 10).
Going to market has four components. In Chapter 10, I will help your company develop all four as a part of your go-to-market customer-centric mindset.

Tie It All Together: Be The One in Ten That Thrives! (Chapter 11).
It's a process: building your great idea into a sustainable business is a huge undertaking and not for the faint of heart. In Chapter 11, we'll review our guideposts—the eight concepts of the customer-centric mindset. These will be the indicators that light your way on the path to revenue.

> *"Good marketing makes the company look smart.*
> *Great marketing makes the customer feel smart."*
> – Joe Chernov[7]

I look forward to leading you through this journey. Let's get started.

3

UNDERSTANDING YOUR CUSTOMERS' MINDSET

> Every part of a business stands to benefit from insights into the customer mindset."[1]

– Geoff Galat

Rodney[2] was a smart, tough leader of a start-up, whose mission became his life's passion: decreasing gun violence and making urban communities safer.

He is CEO of a company that offers public safety solutions to metro police departments across the country. A decade before appointing Rodney CEO, the company had developed an innovative, real-time gunshot detection system. The systems had not gained widespread acceptance, however, mainly because their business model involved selling expensive capital equipment to cities with tight budgets.

Rodney changed the business model to a more affordable, pay-as-you-go proposition–software-as-a-service (SaaS). It was a brilliant move that showed his understanding of their intended customer.

Solving A Life-And-Death Issue

Rodney hoped changing the business model would spur revenue growth. Thirty cities deployed the original offering in the US, but adoption then stalled. Rodney's short-term goal was to double his customer base in less than two years, but gaining market traction was challenging.

He realized that the company's focus on technology made the eyes of city officials glaze over. The company's pure tech-speak made it difficult to grasp the benefits of real-time gunshot detection. Talking technology-algorithms and sound waves would not persuade prospective customers to adopt the solution. Rodney knew he needed to shift the focus to the resulting benefits.

That's when his recruiter contacted me. Rodney knew that I had worked at Regis McKenna, known for marketing technology solutions with a focus on customer benefits.

We agreed that career public safety officials are not likely to embrace technology for the sake of technology. It was their mission—to serve the community—that interested them. To appeal to police chiefs and mayors, we had to focus on customer benefits of decreased gun violence in their communities.

Reducing Urban Gun Violence: Not the Job of Techies

"Theresa", said Rodney, "I believe we can double the customer base if we highlight the benefits of real-time gunshot detection."

I knew he was right.

"Agreed, but this won't be easy. Your tech-centric organization has to think differently about what they offer. If I were to join your team, we'd need to elevate end-user benefits above the technology story." He agreed, and we started down this path together.

When deployed, Rodney's urban solution could detect gunfire in any metro area and send an alert within sixty seconds to police. This alert included vital information, such as the time, number of rounds fired, and GPS location of gunfire, which enabled first responders to arrive on the scene quickly to apprehend criminals, aid injured victims, interview witnesses, and collect evidence.

Elected officials were not interested in risking either their budgets or their reputations on unknown technologies—the stakes were too high. But, those same prospects *were* impressed when hearing their peers talk about decreased gun violence and improved rates of criminal prosecution.

For police chiefs and mayors to adopt and deploy new solutions, they needed proof of the benefits and well-established references. They needed to know that the technology was effective, and that many other cities had already been successful in reducing gun violence by deploying this solution.

Gaining every new customer required the endorsement of prior customers in the form of data-backed proof points and testimonial stories about actual benefits realized by actual police departments.

This makes sense on a broader scale, too. You and I likely look at customer reviews of books, products, and services before purchasing. Social proof is powerful.

As head of marketing for this client, I developed the initial positioning and messaging. We told our impactful story through a compelling website, collateral, and advertising. A high-impact corporate video featured the police chief and several officials from a major US city discussing how to reduce gun violence.

All new materials reflected this positioning, reinforced the messaging, and promoted our powerful solution.

At Rodney's request, I created a comprehensive marketing program for this risk-averse customer segment, based on actual gunshot data we had detected, classified, and archived.

"Proven-use" cases documented declines in gun violence in referenceable metro areas and offered peer testimonials. We wove essential data-backed proof into all our programs, and we published several editions of the *Gunfire Index*.

These books included charts and graphs with aggregated before-and-after data from our actual customers, as well as quotes from police chiefs, mayors, citizens, and elected officials about actual decreases in incidents of gun violence.

The *Gunfire Index* highlighted stories from ten cities. Our company gave the *Index* to prospects and to the press, at no charge to showcase results experienced by cities that had deployed these solutions.

To reach this group successfully and double our customer base, we used a proof-based, referenced-based approach. That gave police chiefs the assurance they needed to feel comfortable deploying the product in their city. Perceived risk took a back seat, compared to the benefits enjoyed by our customers.

For this target customer, we had to highlight benefits, not technology.

We emphasized the outcomes: decreased gun violence, improved conviction rates, the ability to gather more evidence, interview more witnesses, and save more lives.

Testimonial stories coming from peers in other metro police departments won over our next customer, the next one, and then the one after that.

Two factors helped make us successful in that market. First, we changed the business model from a capital equipment purchase to a SaaS subscription service contract. The subscription model was less risky for the customer. If we installed their system, we could ensure performance and also capture gunshot data. (Later analysis on that data demonstrated the decrease in gunfire so it was a win-win.) Second, we created benefit-based messaging using plenty of peer testimonials. Both of these were needed to address a risk-averse customer category.

Segmenting Based On Technology Adoption Mindsets

The case study above illustrates an important point about customers' adoption of new technology. Customer attitude toward adopting new, disruptive technology is significant, because it requires us to change (disrupt) the current way of doing things.

> *For some customers, change means risk. It's scary, and is seen as a* negative. *For others, change is an exciting opportunity, perceived as a* positive.

In Geoffrey A. Moore's classic book on technology marketing, *Crossing the Chasm: Marketing and Selling Disruptive Products to Mainstream Customers*, he explains the technology-adoption life cycle and points out its importance for anyone marketing technology-based solutions.

Crossing the Chasm is generally regarded as the Bible for bringing innovative technology solutions to progressively larger markets. This model is called the technology adoption life cycle curve. Understanding this concept points to the need to adapt messaging based on the mindset of your target market, and makes a big difference in your choice of marketing strategy.

THE TECHNOLOGY ADOPTION LIFE CYCLE

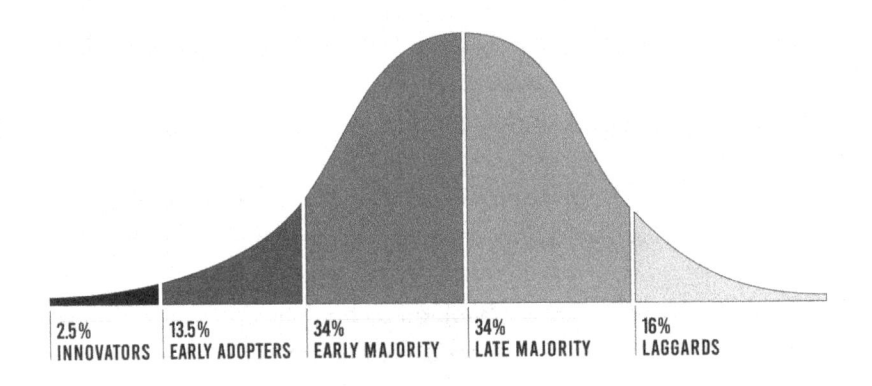

| 2.5% | 13.5% | 34% | 34% | 16% |
| INNOVATORS | EARLY ADOPTERS | EARLY MAJORITY | LATE MAJORITY | LAGGARDS |

*New technology is embraced and adopted in stages.
Like profiles define the stages on a continuum of target market segments.
Corresponding psychographic and social profiles enable us to market to each segment effectively.*

GRAPHIC WITH THE PERMISSION OF GEOFFREY MOORE

The customers in each market segment embrace technology products for different reasons, at varying paces, with distinct considerations in mind.

They have wildly different *attitudes* toward technology adoption.

Understanding the mindset of your target market segment enables one to adapt messaging to suit that mindset. That, in turn, will improve your marketing effectiveness.

These customer-centric concepts are a useful foundation for marketing strategy. They empower us to understand the mindset of our customers, so we can communicate with them and sell to them more effectively.

Revenue growth comes from winning over and successfully serving ever larger markets.

For this discussion about technology products, a **market** is a grouping of actual and potential customers for a set of products or services. These customers have a common set of wants or needs, and reference each other when making buying decisions. The most effective

THE PATH TO REVENUE

marketing strategy is customer-centric—developed to resonate with your target customer, based on their attitude toward adopting new technology.

Your ability to advance from one market to the next larger market segment, adapting your messaging and your marketing strategy along the way, is vital to getting your company on the path to revenue. In fact, that concept is the theory behind the "chasm." Early markets, in which Innovators and Early Adopters readily embrace your technology, must give way to larger, mainstream markets in order for you to realize any substantial revenue growth. Crossing that chasm between the small, early markets and the larger, more profitable mainstream markets is the challenge. Every tech company faces it. It's like a "coming of age."

Your ability to advance from one market to the next, larger market segment is *your path to revenue.*

When this company dropped the tech-speak and began focusing on customer benefits, it made *all* the difference!

We communicated through real-life case studies of known communities: stories were told by police chiefs and mayors, not by our PR team.

The local angle was attractive to local news outlets, as well as TV and newspapers across the country. That snowballed into major stories covered by *USA Today* and a host of other national newspapers. Dozens of major agencies were suddenly writing about decreased gun violence in metro areas, thanks to the benefits of gunshot detection.

That first offering became the market leading option for mitigating illegal urban gunfire. We sold it to public safety officials, such as police chiefs and mayors, who did not build their careers on technology knowledge.

Mayors and police chiefs shared anecdotal testimonials, highlighting the positive changes in their communities.

Same Technology–Different Customer Application–New Revenue Stream

Schools and universities are an entirely different market for gunshot detection. Having your child exposed to gunfire while at school is every parent's worst nightmare.

Sadly, tragedies like these have become all too frequent in America.

The following year, Rodney's company created a second solution based on the same technology, but with a different purpose: real-time identification of active shooter events on school campuses, at universities, in malls, and in other public settings.

With this technology, police could arrive on the scene quickly, armed with data showing where to find the shooter.

There was no other solution available. (Who would have thought there would be a need in the market for a service that identifies an active shooter in real-time?) This SaaS offering was the first solution of its kind, and we marketed it to the innovative customers who eagerly embrace new technology. This segment is *eager* to try innovative technology solutions.

Our target customer for this proprietary solution would be among the first to deploy a technology to address this tragic problem.

Early adopters, like these schools, would not need to review successful testimonials or talk with reference customers.

That was good because there weren't any.

The Technology Adoption Curve

Every alternative technology solution is first adopted by the technology fans who get excited about solving a problem. These customers are *excited* about being the first to have the opportunity to get their hands on this new technology. They know the solution comes with some rough edges—and that's just fine by them. It's a price they're happy to pay.

THE PATH TO REVENUE

Reaching the innovators would not be easy; but it would be possible with the help of the press. Potential customers in the early segments self-identify as they learn about new technologies.

Rodney insisted that we strive for national press coverage. If I had a dollar for every CEO who told me he wanted to be on the cover of a national daily newspaper, I could *own* a national newspaper. This time, however, I agreed that we should make strong press coverage a key objective.

The press were a key component for the launch of this offering. Their coverage would carry our message and help us reach early buyers. It was the innovators who would raise their hands up high, saying, "Let *me* try it, *please!*"

Our marketing goal was to get visibility and highlight how the technology could detect an active shooter in real-time. We made no secret about being the first ones to apply gunshot detection technology to the active shooter scenario.

During the 1999 Columbine High School shootings (some fifteen years prior), first responder SWAT teams reached the victims a full 47 minutes after the first 9-1-1 call came in.

On the heels of the Sandy Hook Elementary School shooting in 2012, when first responders arrived on scene twenty minutes after the first calls, we could urge the press to appeal to the emotions of every single American praying for the end to gun violence.

If we could shortcut the active shooter, we could save the lives of innocent children. It was a hot topic, to be sure, but it was about more than the technology.

When we made the story about the human effects of what the technology *could do*—potentially saving the lives of children across the country—the press was keenly interested.

CBS loved the idea, so we agreed to give them the scoop. They sent a talented, young, ambitious reporter to California to cover our live-fire test at a local school. His finished news piece was any marketers' dream

47

coverage: a full two-minute segment[3] on *The CBS Evening News*, which brought us exposure in hundreds of metro markets across the country.

The CBS Evening News that week drew 7.16 million viewers.[4] Other major television and newspapers picked up on the news, including all the major networks (ABC, NBC, CBS, PBS and Fox TV), major newspapers (*the Washington Post*,[5] *USA Today, the Mercury News, The San Francisco Chronicle*,) online publications (CNET, Bloomberg.com) and vertical publications such as *Campus Safety Magazine*[6], and *Buildings.com.*[7]

A wildly successful product launch announcement jump-started our demand generation efforts. Our goal was to get enough coverage across the country that innovators would self-select and embrace our solution to speed up active shooter response.

Our story was interesting to early adopters of new technology because it was a first-time application of a technology answer to a serious problem.

Success with the Same Technology In Different Market Segments

We bundled this gunshot detection technology into two different offerings.

One solution mitigated urban gun violence and was adopted by the risk-averse early majority customers like police chiefs and civic officials. That target market is practical and depends on well-established peer references and many success stories to be convinced and assured.

The other solution detected gunfire in active shooter scenarios. This offering was adopted by innovators who were desperate to address relatively new problems with new technology.

We marketed these two solutions to two very different target customer groups—or market segments—with very different technology risk tolerance levels. By understanding the mindset of each, we could successfully message the value of each offering and grow revenues for both.

THE PATH TO REVENUE

CROSSING THE CHASM

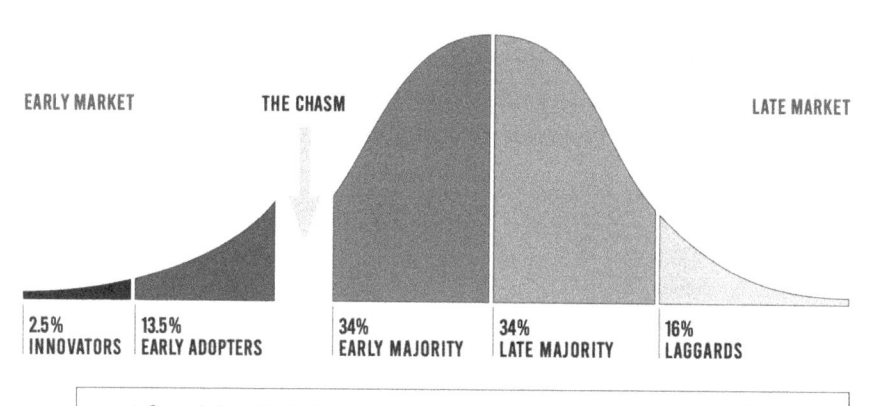

EARLY MARKET	THE CHASM		LATE MARKET

2.5%	13.5%	34%	34%	16%
INNOVATORS	EARLY ADOPTERS	EARLY MAJORITY	LATE MAJORITY	LAGGARDS

1. One solution mitigated urban gun violence and was embraced by some **Early Adopters**.
2. The other solution detected gunfire in active shooter scenarios and was adopted by **Innovators**.

GRAPHIC WITH THE PERMISSION OF GEOFFREY MOORE

We leveraged one technology into two distinct offerings for two separate markets. Different markets means multiple revenue streams. Successfully building revenue streams in both markets required multiple marketing messages and different go-to-market strategies. Note that neither technology has yet crossed the chasm into mainstream markets, thus leaving plenty of room for significant future revenue growth.

Over the next eighteen months, the company more than doubled its customer base to about one hundred metro areas. Having successfully gained that traction, the company launched an IPO that gave them the resources to fund more growth.

PSYCHOGRAPHIC PROFILES: Market Segment Characteristics

Different market segments have different attitudes toward adopting new technologies. Awareness of these mindsets empowers you to market and message effectively.

THERESA MARCROFT

MARKET SEGMENT CHARACTERISTICS

	INNOVATORS	EARLY ADOPTERS	EARLY MAJORITY	LATE MAJORITY	LAGGARDS
RESPONSE TO NEW TECHNOLOGY	Love it! Anything new tech is great.	Likes benefits of new tech, but are not techies.	Likes benefits of new tech, but are not techies at heart.	Not adopting new tech until proven and very compelling.	The last to adopt. Most no longer consider it new tech.
FUNCTION VS. NEW TECHNOLOGY	Tech is of prime interest; function not so important.	Wants to understand the benefits of tech and will buy based on those benefits.	More practical; will wait and see.	Same concerns; will wait and see.	Will buy when truly need functionality and the rest of the world has already embraced it.
PORTION OF TOTAL MARKET	~ 2.5% Very small	~ 13.5% More people.	~ 34% More people.	~ 34% More people.	~ 16% Approx. size of Innovators + Early Adopters.
WHAT PERSUADES THEM MOST?	New shiny toy.	New functionality.	Well established references.	Numerous references + great support + ability to buy from established companies.	There's simply no other alternative now.
"WHOLE PRODUCT" REQUIRED?	No	No	Yes	Yes	Yes

Technology-adoption concepts have been embraced and expanded upon by marketing professionals—both practitioners and professors—many of whom have helped shape my thinking on technology adoption. To meet the market challenges my clients face, I developed the chart above. It helps to think through and develop strategies to best fit each of the target market segments.

©THERESA MARCROFT 2020

APPLICATION

1. Think about how your prospective customers feel about adopting new technologies—will they see your product as a risky disruption to the status quo? or an exciting opportunity?

2. Define each market segment and profile the buyer psyche in each segment. Refer to the two charts in this chapter to help identify where you are now in the market's adoption of your new technology.

3. Hone the value proposition and messaging to target the right people at the right time—new vs proven, "state-of-the-art" vs "industry standard", first on the block to own vs millions of users.

4. Find your target segment on the technology-adoption life cycle. Focus your strategy in line with the needs of that psychographic profile. If you are first enter the market, talking about the unique technology will attract Innovators. If you want to enter a late majority market, you must provide proof: industry references and peer testimonials.

5. Apply this concept when choosing means of distribution: select the channels your customer uses. An innovator might download software online, while the late majority user will expect it to be in a slick, professional package at a store like Best Buy.

6. Apply this concept when developing documentation. An innovator will never read your product documentation, while your late majority user requires a quick-start guide *and* customer support by phone. An innovator wants to hear about the technology, while your late majority user is looking at benefits.

7. Develop a strategy for moving successfully from one market segment to the next, adapting your customer-centric value proposition, messaging, and product as needed along the way.

FINAL THOUGHTS

The technology-adoption life cycle concepts should be top of mind when one sets out to define a company's marketing strategy—characterize each segment of the market by a mindset and market any product or service with the customer perspective in mind.

> *The technology-adoption life cycle concepts should be the foundation for both your marketing strategy and your messaging.*

Segment buyers into like-minded market groups and offer them value to meet their needs, while remaining consistent with their attitudes toward new technologies, and then message accordingly.

Understand the mindset of your customer. Something new could be an exciting opportunity (for an Innovator) or it could be a risky, unproven disruption to 'the way we do things here' (for a Laggard).

Your message will resonate best with the target customer when you understand their mindset toward new technologies. Recognize the customer's mindset and then form messaging and proof points accordingly.

The mindset (i.e., excited vs skeptical) makes all the difference in whether your messaging, value statement *and product* will be well received. You must know your customers' mindset and understand their view on the adoption of new technology.

Remember, crossing the chasm is not easy, but it's possible if you understand and stay focused on your customers' mindset.

Popping the champagne in victory is always a goal, but as Chapter 4 shows, it will only happen if you properly coordinate the branding, positioning, and messaging.

4

COMMUNICATING VALUE WITH CUSTOMER-CENTRIC MESSAGING

> If you're going to grab the microphone, you'd better know what you want to say!"
>
> —Oft-heard remark in the lunchroom at Regis McKenna PR

David, a former director of security with the federal government, was a code-cracker turned CEO. A Southern gentleman and a likeable guy, he was a security expert with deep technical expertise in encryption, data protection, and authentication. A leading network security company appointed David CEO.

The sales team was equipped with superior customer relations skills and deep product knowledge. That enabled them to help their customers choose and implement solutions from a range of network security products—a profitable, albeit highly specialized, business. David's dilemma was that his salespeople spoke in an encrypted code that prospects just could not crack.

THERESA MARCROFT

Taking New Products to Market

David had big plans for expanding his product line into several new areas. Two acquisitions were in the pipeline and two new products were in development. However, he knew introducing new products to the market was not the job of sales. No one on his staff was skilled at new product introductions, launch messaging, and competitive positioning. David decided to "get marketing," and that's when his recruiter called me.

David and I sat together in his office for the first time one summer day in sunny Silicon Valley. He explained his plans for adding more security solutions to his growing portfolio of high-performance encryption appliances and solutions.

He drew two lines on his whiteboard, one vertical and one horizontal, making four squares. In the first square, he noted the legacy products that had been their bread and butter for a decade. Soon, they would add two other security solutions—virtual private networks (VPNs) and public key infrastructure (PKI)—to the portfolio.

Further into the future, wireless security solutions would complement their hardware and software solutions. Creating a story that could successfully unite this scattered product line to create one brand would be a challenge. Building a brand starts from the inside, I explained to David. He smiled his famous, confident smile, showing that he knew we could do it.

Getting Started

In my first week with the company, my own (admittedly unscientific) poll asked a few dozen employees, "What does our company do?" The hope was to have a variety of employees explain the business to me in their own words. What does this company offer their customers? What problems does this company solve? The question asked twenty-six times yielded twenty-six answers including, "Something computer-related," "Some type of security," "Corporate networking," and "I have no idea!"

This was far from ideal.

The most successful brand-building adventures require that *all* employees—from the reception desk to the corner office and everyone in-between— know, understand, believe and can articulate the company's mission. Each person should have a sentence on the tips of their tongues to explain what the company does and how their customers benefit.

David's company did not have a simple way to articulate the value they provide in their security solutions. They dove straight into tech-speak on the first slide of the corporate presentation. Non-engineers were left scratching their heads—and that was *before* they added other new products.

What was the common thread? David's planned expansion of the solution set would be an opportunity to craft a brilliant story and position the company for growth. The next step would be to uncover and articulate this company's actual value in terms of the benefits provided to the customer.

Customer-Centric Value

We had to base positioning on the value delivered to customers. The message had to resonate with the consumer. But what was our unique value? What was our message?

To answer that question, my marketing team had to enlist the help of the sales team. After all, sales was on the front lines.

They were the ones who talked with customers every day and knew their requirements and frustrations. Input from the sales team would be key to crafting a message that would resonate best with our customers.

We teamed up and asked questions: What did the customer want to accomplish by implementing our network security solutions? Why did people buy our products? What were the challenges that faced their business that prompted them to look into new solutions? Why did they like our products? What was *not* being provided that they wanted? Why did they want it? How did they use these solutions? How well did this portfolio of security offerings meet their needs?

Articulating a Customer-Centric Core Benefit

By asking these questions, we learned what customers wanted. We learned that our encryption solutions were great at meeting their needs for network security. Additionally, the product roadmap promised to satisfy even more of their business security needs.

We gave them the ability to secure their business anywhere—inside or outside the firewall, on the desktop, via mobile devices, across distributed corporate networks, and at all the remote offices. Some applications called for hardware solutions; others required software. David's company could meet *all* of those needs. *That* was the real value to the customer:

> *Anywhere and anyway you want to do business securely, we've got you covered. Securing eBusiness. That's what we do.*

We developed our value proposition around that claim. The value proposition format I recommend is as follows:

POSITIONING CLAIM EXAMPLE

TEMPLATE	OUR UNIQUE VALUE PROPOSITION
FOR ___	FOR corporate F500 and government agencies.
WHO ___	WHO need to secure all aspects of their businesses.
WE OFFER ___	WE OFFER a comprehensive family of solutions to secure eBusiness.
THAT PROVIDE ___	THAT PROVIDE highest level data security to protect all business communications and transactions.
OUR SOLUTIONS ___	OUR SOLUTIONS (unique differentiation) are based on the highest level of cryptographic-based security standards and delivered in software, hardware, and wireless solutions.

Positioning defines how you want your audience to think about your product or service; while *messaging* is a set of specific statements crafted to communicate your value to your customer while establishing and reinforcing your positioning. You must base both on the benefits of your product—not technology, features, or functionality.

> *Securing eBusiness. That's what we do. We will secure your business anywhere—on the corporate network, inside or outside the firewall, on a desktop, in any remote location, or via any mobile device. We will secure your business in the way that makes sense—with a software solution, a hardware appliance, a wireless solution, or a hybrid combination, in the USA or abroad, today or tomorrow.*

Thus, "*Securing eBusiness*" became the prime point of our value proposition—our brand promise to the customer—in words that the customer used. It became the top layer of our messaging and it led to a discussion about how to address each customer's security needs.

The *Securing eBusiness* message was elegantly simple. The next level points were, too. Everyone in the company could remember and articulate this, not only in a corporate presentation but when visitors walked into the lobby or over beers on Friday evenings.

Though articulation always suffers by the end of Happy Hour.

MESSAGING HIERARCHY TEMPLATE

BRAND PROMISE: SECURING E-BUSINESS			
ANY PLACE	ANYWHERE ON THE NETWORK	ANY LOCATION	ANY WAY THAT MAKES SENSE
CORPORATE DATA CENTER	INSIDE OR OUTSIDE FIREWALL	MAIN OFFICE	HARDWARE
ANY DESKTOP ON NETWORK	AT CORPORATE	GLOBAL BRANCH OFFICES	SOFTWARE
ANY MOBILE DEVICE	REMOTELY	REMOTE LOCATIONS	WIRELESS SOLUTIONS

Everyone in the company understood this messaging and could remember it. Soon we started to benefit from the brand-building synergy that's created when everyone is saying the same thing and using identical words.

It was the messaging that the company had been sorely missing.

Over and over, in thousands of conversations with tens of thousands of people, we realized the messaging was spot on.

Continued Success Based on Customer-Centric Value

Strong branding unified the product line as it expanded over the coming year. The path to revenue was well-paved; the story held together. The branding made sense, and the positioning was compelling and relevant to the customer.

People inside and outside of the company understood and remembered our messaging. (If I had conducted that same poll again, I would have heard the same answer twenty-six times: "We secure eBusiness!")

THE PATH TO REVENUE

Our offering was competitive and differentiated. We now had an identity as the folks who "secure eBusiness", and that was something on which we could hang our hats. The pace of our revenue growth picked up.

We were creating jobs at a time when unemployment in Silicon Valley reached an all-time low. People wouldn't answer recruiters' calls and wouldn't show up for interviews. Starting bonuses were exorbitant. We needed to stand out—not only as a provider of great security solutions, but also as a desirable potential employer.

So, we decided to have fun with this.

Our head of communications, Gene Carozza, worked with our advertising agency to develop a TV commercial that showed off our new identity—securing eBusiness anywhere, anytime, in any way. It was shown during the six o'clock news. The "Do What You Want To Do!" ad was a daring and funny head-turner.

While the Isley Brothers sang their funk Motown hit, "It's Your Thing" ("It's your thing, do what you wanna do…"), our thirty-second spot featured young and old people doing "their thing."

The spot interspersed many elements: black and white images with colorful ones, city with countryside, buttoned down folks, Berkeley hippies, and teens at '60s dance parties.

It even featured an octogenarian *getting down.*

And hopefully getting back up.

It grabbed attention. It got people talking about this fun place to work. And it communicated the message: We will secure your business—any business, anywhere, any time, on any platform. So, do what you want to do! Securely.

Mission accomplished.

The company unified the product line offering under one branding umbrella. It got everyone on the same page when they explained their offering to others. It gave the company a simple story that each employee could believe in and remember.

Each sales rep could trust in the branding story to launch into any product story they wanted to tell (or sell). They could talk about software, hardware, services, warranties, today's solutions, or tomorrow's roadmap.

All of this work helped transform the company. What was once an organization driven by engineering was now market- and customer-driven. Sales presentations that once opened with security protocols and encryption algorithms now began with the benefits of securing our customers' businesses. Now we were talking about our solutions in a unified and compelling way, which was resonating with our customers like never before.

Conducting business with some personality was rare in the network security industry. It made the company feel approachable.

Job applications started streaming in. We had slightly demystified network security and everyone had fun. That enabled this company to carve out a competitive space in the market to drive revenue growth.

The newly unified branding and strong, consistent messaging made the company very attractive—to customers and to employees. This played a large role in the company receiving an amazing offer of acquisition.

Positioning

Positioning is a hefty subject. People have written volumes of book—tomes, actually—on positioning. By definition, positioning is competitive. It's the space you occupy in the customer's mind. It's what you want people to remember; it's *why* they choose your solution over a different one. For that reason, it will serve you well to give the customer, and the market, a framework for thinking about your offering.

Here's a straightforward way to approach this. A brand-positioning map comprises attributes important to your target audience. By placing

THE PATH TO REVENUE

your brand, and your competitors, on your map, you'll see who's more competitive in a certain area over the rest.

Imagine you are about to buy a new computer. The reason you have dozens of choices is that each model has different strengths and weaknesses. You have to decide what's important to YOU.

This is an admittedly simplified competitive landscape. Maybe you view choices this way; maybe you don't. Maybe you start with the concept that price is THE most important factor—in which case you'll be looking at options on the left half of this matrix. Maybe price means nothing to you and functionality/power is everything—in which case you'll be looking at the top half of the matrix.

COMPUTER PURCHASE EXAMPLE

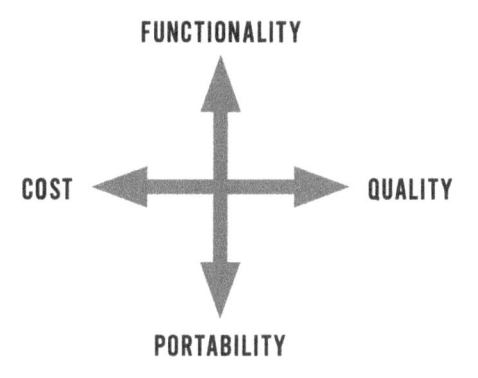

```
            FUNCTIONALITY
                 ↑
                 |
    COST ←———————+———————→ QUALITY
                 |
                 ↓
            PORTABILITY
```

> *Be intentional about developing your positioning.*
> *Allow it to influence your messaging as you develop the messaging hierarchy or pyramid.*

Now you have the markers—the guideposts—of your positioning. In this example, these are functionality, portability, quality, and cost. Play with that. See how far you can push the envelope. Don't be afraid to get outrageous with your positioning. Shocking people gets their attention. If your outrageous claim is based in truth, you'll get away with it. Here are some examples:

- Lay's: "Bettcha Can't Eat Just One."
- Bounty: "The Quicker Picker-Upper"
- State Farm: "Like a Good Neighbor, State Farm is There."
- L'Oreal: "Because You're Worth It"

Based on value, each of these outrageous claims opens the door to a story the company can tell. The story the company *wants to* tell. Facts support *the core* of these claims, even the outrageous ones.

> "Outrageous positioning is a wink between a credible company and its supportive customers—it is not hucksterism."[1] *–Guy Kawasaki*

APPLICATION

1. Define the customer problem you are *uniquely* ready, willing, and able to solve. Be clear and concise when describing what it is you represent.

2. Craft your **positioning** so it reflects the target customer's reality—their view of alternative solutions and the unique value you offer. This will ensure that your positioning is true and compelling.

3. Ensure that your unique position differs from competitors in a way that's *meaningful* to your customer (not in some obscure way that only your engineers care about!).

4. Distill your **messaging** down to the lowest common denominator: *Securing eBusiness*. The simplest form should still be factual and memorable. This is the top level of your messaging hierarchy.

5. Complete your messaging hierarchy by building out the next 2-4 levels, adding more information and proof points as you go into more detail.

6. Make sure everyone in your company knows what your **brand** stands for and why. This increases the likelihood that everyone is singing the same song and using the same words. And it gives you the benefit of synergy.

7. Relentlessly reinforce your branding and communicate your positioning through consistent messaging. Repeat the message often. You will grow very weary of hearing this mantra long before the usefulness of the message is worn out.

8. Be willing to change as the competitive landscape demands. Just don't allow every shifting wind to alter your top level messaging. Stay the course.

FINAL THOUGHTS

The starting point is *always* the customer.

Interesting positioning, strong strategic branding, a meaningful value proposition and clear, convincing messaging resonate with your customer.

Branding is who you are— *the company who secures eBusiness.*

Your brand, when built on a value statement that's credible, opens every conversation. The brand is *the* starting point for all conversations.

Positioning sets you apart from the competition and gives the customer a reason to buy from *you*. It's also, by definition, dynamic. It changes as the market changes, and as the competitive landscape changes.

Messaging introduces the needed information about how this offering meets customer needs. To be sure, it requires detailed, technical data to make a buy decision about complex products, but the high-level messaging sets the stage and gives a context for the rest.

Like positioning, messaging is competitive and dynamic. The simpler, the better.

A short, simple message is powerful!. One of the most iconic marketing slogans in history was just three syllables long:

Nike's *Just Do It*.

This campaign began in 1988 is still going strong.

Intentionally, the words lack context (Do *What?*) and are intended to let consumers apply the words to their own situation. For a brand like Nike, whose aim is to inspire training, working out, and self-improvement, the motivational slogan works.

"Securing eBusiness" is much more targeted, yet perfectly conveys how this company can meet their customers' security needs.

The tip of the messaging pyramid is just as important as the base—maybe more so. Allow it to open and close every customer conversation.

In the big picture of customer-centric marketing, all of this fits together to optimize sales and put your company on the path to revenue.

> "Less is more. Keeping it simple takes time and effort."
> *–Jeff Bullas*[1]

Chapter 5 will highlight how one company had to adjust their strategies as e-commerce took its seat at the table.

5

EMPOWERING SALES WITH CUSTOMER-CENTRIC CONTENT

> Give your audience *knowledge* (not biased marketing), and you set up a powerful foundation for future sales."[1]
>
> –Ryan Floyd, VC, Storm Ventures

James scratched his head. He faced a puzzle, a riddle, a true conundrum that many business leaders face when running technology companies.

His media tech company was in the digital advertising marketing space. The industry's simplistic nickname, 'ad tech,' belied the complexity of the offering.

"Theresa, if you can figure out how we can present this more effectively so that our customers grasp it more quickly, that would be tremendously helpful," James confided to me.

The company was a start-up of high-intellect professionals, intent on leveraging offline data (such as demographics) for better online marketing.

In each initial, high-level introduction, James' sales team faced several significant challenges. It was a complicated product, featuring hard-to-explain technology and a highly intricate back-end process.

Being data geeks, James and his team spoke effortlessly about their technology and assumed everyone could see the value. There was vast potential to improve the accuracy of online advertising and targeting. However, some potential customers didn't understand the real advantages they offered. The technology was tough to articulate, as was the value proposition.

As a result, the first conversation with potential customers rarely went smoothly.

Uncovering Customer-Centric Core Benefits

The team needed a message that would resonate with prospects and highlight customer benefits. My aim for this client—just as it is for your company—was to uncover the core value proposition. We then had to describe this value proposition in a compelling story, which the sales team would be comfortable re-telling prospects.

Working with James, his team, and the executives, the plan was to take the company through market and competitive analyses to shine a spotlight on the core value.

That would provide the base for our corporate and product messaging, which we would then weave into much-needed sales tools.

Empowering the sales team with effective selling tools always starts with customer-centric content. The value proposition is like a marketing team's morning coffee: it kicks off the process and equips them with the ammunition they need to complete the task.

The value proposition must be both factual and one that resonates meaningfully with customers.

Finding Your Unique Benefit

To discover a company's unique strengths, look at industry trends, the competitive landscape, and gaps in rival offerings. Then, identify and state your unique and interesting value proposition. For this client, it was enabling online advertisers to efficiently find, and market to, their ideal target customers.

James' company could *create online audiences*—effectively, accurately, efficiently, and successfully.

Once you think you can clearly articulate this benefit—test, test, and test again. Try it out on current clients and prospects. Test it on everyone with whom you interact. Ask them to repeat back to you what they heard. Do they see that as a benefit? If so, why? How will that help them? How will they use that capability? What impact will it have on their business? Why have they not been able to accomplish that with other products?

All of this dialogue will give you the needed information to either confirm or tweak your draft messaging.

This process helped my ad tech client develop a succinct brand promise:

Unlocking Big Data to Power Digital Marketing. This made sense to everyone who heard it, so we knew we were on to something. And it didn't hurt that Big Data was a trendy buzzword in venture capital circles.

The company began to benefit from the synergy of all their teams using the messaging. Customers found this story very compelling. Beyond the high-level brand promise, the messaging explained the use of offline data to inform data-driven marketing, and that resonated quite well with serious digital marketers.

The Core Benefit, Key Value Offered

This brief message—*create online audiences*—served as the tip of the messaging pyramid. *Unlocking Big Data to Power Digital Marketing* became the new tagline. And it was effective because people intuitively understood what it means to create online audiences. Right away they want to know *how* that's done.

As we discussed in the last chapter, the highest-level message should be strong and flexible enough to open any conversation.

Create online audiences.

Whether it's a first sales meeting with a new prospect, or an annual account review with a long-time customer, that message could open up a discussion with our customer's CEO, CFO, or technical lead. It was the main message on our web site home page and it could also be used to open doors to the press.

It opens and closes *any* conversation.

Role-Specific Customer-Centric Messaging

The average B2B customer has several people in different roles involved in making and/or approving the purchase decision. It was important to consider the various roles of the various people involved in the buying and renewal decisions.

We took care to develop a messaging hierarchy specific to each distinct buyer.

This exercise is often referred to as developing "customer personas." "Based on research and analysis, customer personas are important because they help us to identify and understand our target customers. Knowing their attributes and characteristics, responsibilities, and other traits enables us to market to them effectively.

Back to "*Create online audiences:* unlock big data to power digital marketing." One set of messaging was crafted directly toward technical digital marketers. A less-detailed version was prepared for CIOs which

THE PATH TO REVENUE

included information specific to their interests. A third version, prepared for the purchasing department and CFOs, included the ROI story.

These role-specific versions of the messaging still start and end with the same simple message—the one you find at the top of the messaging pyramid: *Create Online Audiences, Unlock Big Data to Power Digital Marketing.* That highest level point doesn't change.

The sales team could now tell a compelling story that clearly articulated their value in the crowded and otherwise confusing ad tech space. Toward the end of my consulting project there, James was elated.

He said to me, "My sales team is excited about using more straightforward, less technical talk to describe our business. This will help us open doors faster, shorten the sales cycle, and close more deals."

Standing On Its Own

The next year, James' company secured a multi-million dollar round of funding. The last time I checked, they had significantly accelerated their annual revenue run rate, with an expanded customer base maintaining a very low customer churn rate.

I expect the company will continue to grow at a steady pace, securing their spot as one of the 10% of start-ups that creates a successful business.

They are clearly on the path to revenue.

The New Content Marketing

As B2B buyers become more sophisticated in their independent research, there is a strong thirst for content that educates and informs, rather than sells. An overwhelming majority (93 percent) want content that has less of a sales pitch, while 94 percent want access to content without having to fill out long lead gen forms.[2]

To meet their needs, it's marketing's job to serve up content that provides more educational information, data, and statistics. This is the idea behind **content marketing** today. Content marketing *educates* people with the information they seek, rather than by explicitly selling to them.

But that's not enough.

Yes, people seek straightforward information. But the genius happens when you *entertain* at the same time you educate.

> *Content marketing is the development, creation, and online publication of valuable, relevant, and consistent content that people want to read (or watch) and share.*

Great content serves people because it entertains and informs, which leads to increased engagement. THAT is why content marketing is so important—engagement leads to growth.

The Power of Video

If a picture is worth a thousand words, a short video is worth a million.

Some fabulous examples include the videos "So yeah, We Tried Slack," and Adobe's "Click, Baby, Click."

Both of them are short, entertaining, videos that showcase their value propositions (Slack's workplace collaboration and Adobe's marketing analytics) in a way that's fun to watch.

According to Bandwatch.com, 500 hours of video are uploaded to YouTube every minute, which equates to 720,000 hours of video being uploaded every day.[3]

Over 1 billion hours of YouTube videos are watched daily, more than Netflix and Facebook videos combined.[4] People share content that is fun, different, shocking, or otherwise unique. When they share your content, you have multiplied your sales force.

And the video-sharing sales force works for free.

THE PATH TO REVENUE

Keep doing that and growth will follow.

You can list many kinds of content under the label of content marketing. Content marketing is about much more than blogging, although that is one very solid approach. Content has evolved and exploded. There are many kinds of content available to choose and use at the right time in the sales cycle. They include:

- **Audio**—podcasts, interviews, webinars, keynote speeches
- **Video**—YouTube, custom corporate videos, customer testimonials, ads
- **Print**—web copy, press releases, case studies, e-books, white papers, e-mail campaigns, blogs, tweets and posts

B2B buyers say they rely heavily on white papers (82 percent), webinars (78 percent), and case studies (73 percent) to make purchasing decisions. Close behind are e-books (67 percent), infographics (66 percent), and blog posts (66 percent).[5]

Consumers share infographics about twenty times more often than a typical blog post and have a higher likelihood of getting picked up by other online publications.[6]

I created this infographic to celebrate the 15-year anniversary of my MarketSavvy consulting business. It was on the web site and in my newsletter.

15 YEARS OF SERVING MY CEO CLIENTS

15 — VETERAN CMO
Led marketing in "interim CMO" role.

14 — MAJOR PRODUCT LAUNCHES
Took new products to market successfully.

12 — PUBLISHED ARTICLES
Wrote and placed major articles in key target publications and national newspapers.

8 — COMPANY LAUNCHES
Positioned and launched new companies into the market.

7 — CORPORATE WEB SITES
Corporate web sites based on behavioral insights and decision making.

6 — CORPORATE ACQUISITIONS
Strategically positioned companies to be successfully acquired.

5 — NET PROMOTER
Conducted customer surveys to understand and rate customer satisfaction.

3 — INITIAL PUBLIC OFFERINGS
Led three clients to successful IPOs.

3 — AWARD WINNING VIDEOS
Storytelling videos earned three **ADDY awards** — peer reviewed recognition of excellence in video.

2 — THOUGHT LEADERSHIP
Wrote 2 books publishing data analysis and findings.

1 — NEW PRODUCT INTRO
On **CBS Evening News** feature story covering a new product introduction. This 2+minute segment reached millions of households in thousands of cities.

GLOBAL RESULTS — CLIENT NAMED
Fastest growing company in Asia, Best marketing in India, Best pan-European Awareness Campaign.

©THERESA MARCROFT 2020

Traditional Marketing

Historically, marketing and sales functions have been organized serially: the first half of the sales cycle belonged to marketing to generate, pre-qualify, and nurture leads. Marketing would build brand awareness and generate demand. . . and then hand off the most qualified opportunities to the sales department for in-person pursuit. The second half of the "sales cycle" belonged to sales, to further qualify prospects, close the deal and ensure that post-sales support was in place.

Today, this "marketing first, sales second" arrangement is no longer.

Key Changes In B2B Buying

Three significant transitions in the B2B buying process demand have changed the role of marketing. These new realities have implications for how we think about content marketing, how we empower and enable sales, and how we adapt our content.

First, the buying process has moved online. Sales reps are no longer the *only* channel to customers; they are *one of many channels* to reach the customer.

No longer are we on the front lines of a linear process. No longer does marketing manage the customer during the first half of the buyer's journey and sales manage the second half. Information flows from many directions and is consumed by new and varied participants in the buying decision.

The "handoff" from marketing to sales, and from digital to in-person is blurred. Understanding this is more important than ever.

Content marketing is the key to being successful in that new dynamic.

We must create ever-more interesting content, as our prospects now turn to online research before ever engaging with a sales rep. According to Forrester, 60% of buyers would rather not communicate with sales reps as their primary information source, and 68% prefer to do online research on their own.[7] *Forbes* confirms this, noting that B2B customers today progress over 70% of the way through the decision-making process before ever engaging a sales rep.[8]

Given the new buying process, our marketing job is to make online content not only highly informative and educational, but also entertaining and memorable. It must be share-worthy to entice prospects and keep them coming back for more.

Like children to a dessert table.

This is all very different from the serial process we used to know.

In addition, we must ensure that content is aligned across in-person and digital channels. This enables us to support customers in the way they prefer to research and buy today. This is now a matrixed process involving multiple people gathering information in parallel, both online and in person.

Second, the buying process has become more complicated. According to research group Gartner, "The typical buying group for a complex B2B solution involves six to ten decision makers, each armed with four or five pieces of information they've gathered independently."[9] The buy decision today involves more people, and each of them can now do their own research, easily and independently.

We marketers need to adapt, too.

THE BUYER'S JOURNEY MATRIX™

	I.T. DIRECTOR	CIO OR CISO	PURCHASING MGR	FINANCE CFO	CEO
AWARENESS	✔	✔	✔	✔	✔
INTEREST	✔	✔	✔	✔	✔
NEED/INTENT	✔	✔	✔	✔	✔
EVALUATION	✔	✔	✔	✔	✔
PURCHASE	✔	✔	✔	✔	✔

Organize your content assets and map them to today's buyer journey. Map out the pieces by target role and by stage of the sales funnel to ensure a full suite of content. For example, content designed for the IT director at the 'interest' stage of the sale differs greatly from content designed to gain the approval of the CFO at the purchase stage.

©THERESA MARCROFT 2020

THE PATH TO REVENUE

We need to deliver content to prospective buyers in each role that has influence over the final buying decision—because there's almost always multiple people involved in the B2B buy.

We usually need to have several contacts sign off—including the technical influencers, the budget owner, and the purchasing department. In addition, you must convince others, such as the CFO and sometimes the CEO (depending on the size of the purchase) about why you are an appropriate vendor with a relevant product. Often, these executives have the ability to veto a purchase with which they're not comfortable. They often do their own research and approach the topic from unique perspectives. We must deliver content that's effective for each of those different roles.

We need to satisfy *each* of these constituents.

Third, more Millennials are making B2B purchases. We use the term 'Millennial', aka Gen Y, to refer to the demographic born between 1981 and 1996. They are the children of the 'Baby Boomers.

According to a recent report by Google, almost 50 percent of buyers doing the initial research—the ones selecting a short list of vendors to invite to the last stages of the process—were Millennials, and that number continues to grow.[10]

According to Google, 71 percent of purchase research begins with a generic query.[11] Prospects are looking for solutions to their problem first; they are *not* searching for your product or company name. Where do you show up in that process?

Furthermore, 70 percent of B2B buyers watch a video during the buying process.[12] Does your content plan include video assets?

Millennials grew up with a cell phone and, to this day, this device rarely leaves their hands. They live on social media—it's second nature to them. If Millennials are the ones making the buy decisions and they are doing 100 percent of their research online, then marketing must adapt to be effective.

Or buyers will find a competitor that will.

This accounts for the rise and importance of social media in B2B marketing and the birth of an entire industry providing tools and services around social media marketing.

Social Media Marketing Tools

Digital marketing has become an important part of today's corporate marketing department. B2B buyers do their research online before making a purchase. At least 75 percent of B2B buyers conduct research in social channels for products and services before decision time.[13] These social channels carry your message to your target audience. Leverage social media to do your content marketing, or use more traditional means, like printed pieces. Ideally, social media and traditional marketing strategies should work in parallel to augment and reinforce each other.

Take advantage of the many tools that are available now. Spend time getting familiar with the social media tools—for content development, content publication, and for measurement.

Social media management tools are many and varied. The market-leading big names come and go. Search online for the tools that deliver the functionality you need. That said, here's how the tools universe exploded in the last decade.

THE PATH TO REVENUE

EXPLOSION OF SOCIAL MEDIA MARKETING TOOLS

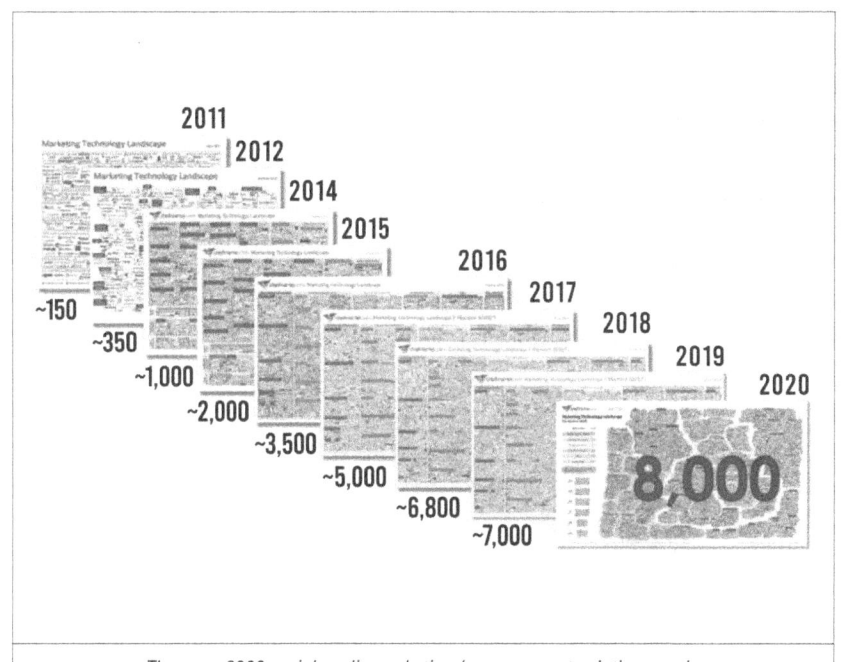

There are 8000 social media marketing / management solutions on the 2020 Marketing Technology Landscape Supergraphic — up from only 150 tools noted back in 2011.

MARKETING TECHNOLOGY LANDSCAPE 2020: MARTECH 5000, COURTESY OF CHIEFMARTEC.COM

Choose tools based on your needs, the size and talent of your team, and whether or not your social media strategy requires collaboration. Some platforms enable you to integrate social accounts, allow bulk scheduling, and include content curation. Others enable brand management and tracking your brand across multiple social channels and the web.

Among the functionality offered:

- Calendars for scheduling and repeating posts
- The ability to audit your SEO efforts
- In-depth analytics
- Reports on your visibility and that of your competitors
- Free subscriptions

Most tools offer a free version, with more value, functionality, and better reporting available at a paid tier.

Carefully select the mix of tools to meet the needs of your department and augment the talent pool you have in place.

One of the enormous challenges facing marketing leaders now is how to assemble the right stack of tools to meet the needs of your team. Determine if they'd rather have several single-purpose tools or a single integrated platform.

The Role of Social Media in Tech Marketing

The current love-fest with social media is entertaining. At best, it is sometimes the perfect choice to get your message out to just the right audience at the right time.

Especially with consumer products.

The favorable tweet or image posted by a big star or influencer can make (or break) an entire brand. In that light, social media can be highly influential, even invaluable.

Just as eating *only* nuts is not a healthy diet, using social media *alone* isn't a sustainable strategy. Social media are part of a multi-faceted communications plan, but it cannot take the place of a well thought-out and comprehensive marketing mix.

There is *so much more* to marketing than social media.

> *Social media is not marketing strategy.*
> *It carries your message for a short-lived moment in the spotlight unless done in context of the larger marketing mix.*

Here's a good way to view the role of social media in tech marketing: use it to build an audience and create a two-way conversation. In order to do that, the focus must be on maximizing engagement and creating compelling content that will lead to a high level of conversion. (It's *much* more strategic than posting or tweeting for the sake of posting and tweeting.)

Social media can be a key component of your marketing strategy and has the most impact when it is part of a coordinated messaging strategy. Your company will enjoy the synergy of all those social media marketing channels working toward the same end.

Once you're in the conversation, then you're in the sales process. You're halfway home. Now let the sales conversation play out, hopefully to a happy ending.

Content Marketing Example: Hubitat.com

One company making smart home products has a target audience of do-it-yourself home improvement enthusiasts. These guys love to tinker around the house on the weekends.

The company leverages many kinds of content to reach their audience, inform them about the product and its uses, and build a following.

Their site is a good example of content marketing: basic information is augmented by an immense library of resources—including many blogs and video tutorials. There are dozens of introductory, advanced, and application-specific videos—all under three minutes so people can quickly see and hear the info they needed. Besides a few dozen videos, the resource section includes written documents.

DIY enthusiasts like to discuss smart home improvements with others and get the latest tips from their friends, so they developed an online community to swap stories and suggestions. There, people with hands-on experience with the product can comment, as well as ask and answer questions for everyone's benefit.

The online community is a vital resource for their customers. People post additional questions as they arise and require answers. Through their frequency, customer questions and feedback indicate which areas need additional collateral and/or videos. There's also a long list of compatible devices and make sure that there are easy links to complementary products one might want to use.

As a quirky testament to the importance of reaching *all* of your audience, the community is also a resource for the smart home enthusiasts who aimed to please their spouse in this process (or at least minimize their objections). The WAF (Wife Acceptance Factor) had a Bigfoot-like status in the community—it was often discussed, and sometimes feared but rarely confronted. Yet, it is so important to the home improvement enthusiasts that it has its own area of content resources.

This vast array of varied content is easy-to-find–all in one place. It empowers new users to get started and provides veteran users with advanced information. Every customer can access the information they are seeking in the format they prefer.

APPLICATION

1. Understand that three significant transitions are changing the role of marketing:

- The buying process has moved online. Know what online resources your customers use.
- The buying process has become more complicated.
- Millennials are making more B2B purchases.

2. Review the Buyer's Journey Matrix and develop your customer personas for each Role. For each potential sale, know which buyer roles will influence the purchase decision and where they are getting their information. Ensure that you have the right content in the right form for the right target at each stage in the sales cycle.

3. Identify gaps in your content offering by gathering feedback on existing tools. As a test, review your content assuming there's never an in-person consultation with your sales professional. Is the online information complete?

4. Assemble and create new content offerings based on the top ten questions that prospects might ask. Consult with the sales team to discover the most frequently asked questions. Ensure you have content to answer these FAQs.

5. Be certain that each piece of content is valuable, educational and informative. Try to make each entertaining so that people want to share. Make them shareable.

6. Ensure that, wherever possible, all content is available in both online and offline formats.

FINAL THOUGHTS

Significant transitions are changing the role of B2B purchasing and therefore B2B marketing. We know that Millennials are making more B2B purchases, so it follows that most buying has moved online, complicating the purchasing process.

Content marketing easily enables the many people involved in the buying process to find needed information that speaks to their individual role-based priorities. It caters to decision-making teams and serves up useful, factual information at the right stage of the sales cycle. It also ensures that the content served is relevant for that role, based on customer personas.

Content marketing strategy also aligns offline and online content, acknowledging that consumption of content can happen anywhere, anytime, by the gamut of players who influence the purchase decision.

Many companies don't acknowledge all the people involved in making, approving or thwarting the buy decision. The 10% of companies that survive the start-up stage understand the B2B buying process. And, they leverage the power of content shared by people other than your sales and marketing teams.

Understanding and embracing these concepts will be a huge step toward planting your feet firmly on the path to revenue.

What if your product creates an entirely new market? Chapter 6 describes why doing so can be the "Autobahn to Profitability."

6

CREATING AND CLAIMING YOUR MARKET

> If you see a bandwagon, it's too late."
>
> –James Goldsmith

Roberto, the soft-spoken brains behind a new start-up, wanted to provide a product that made a difference.

As businesses moved online at breakneck speed, they needed a way to understand online customer behavior. Roberto envisioned providing insightful information that companies could use to better serve their customers and to empower them to run their new online businesses efficiently.

To do that, it was important to understand website visitor behavior and surfer browsing patterns. Website usage statistics have become an essential part of any new webmaster's responsibilities.

At first, analyzing user behavior on a website was a manual process that involved reviewing web server log files and implementing data mining techniques.

Log analysis results were often ambiguous, incomplete—or both—and interpreting site usage data was as difficult as a close-up conversation with your garlic-loving neighbor.

These challenges gave way to the rise of rudimentary software tools with which a webmaster could access raw server statistics, such as gross numbers of hits and visitors. Many of the early log analysis tools were platform-specific, and most were Unix-based.[1] Programs built for Unix are not often credited with user-friendliness.[2]

Roberto's company had developed a new approach to website analysis, based on the needs of online businesses. They gathered and delivered clear information about the site visitor's behavior, from which they could track buyer browsing patterns, as well as determine what information the visitor 'consumed' prior to buying a product online or taking other desired actions.

In short, this approach focused on the customer's needs, much like Trader Joe's does.

Roberto knew his product was brilliant, yet taking it to market was another story altogether. That's when the company decided they needed to add marketing to their small core team of engineers.

The Pivot Point

Roberto and I met for the first time in the warehouse where he had set up shop. We discussed the challenge at hand and I asked him to confirm: "The early tools that exist so far are designed to conduct web-based network traffic monitoring and web server log analysis. Is that right?"

"Yes." He explained further, "Even for the most well-known tools available now, the output comprises raw server statistics, such as gross numbers of hits and visitors."

Through our discussion Roberto, the need became apparent. People were frustrated by tool limitations and the lack of insight gained from using them. Their websites *were* their businesses, and they needed to know more. They required clear and actionable intelligence.

The existing category was "web server log analysis tools," but that was not what we did or wanted to do. It wasn't the category to which Roberto wanted to belong.

More granular data could paint a much bigger picture. It could give large companies the insight they needed into their websites and their online businesses.

Upon joining this six-man team, I guided them through a positioning project. Together, we decided to create a new category for "high-end website analysis," an approach our customers could use to optimize their online businesses.

Early customers were Fortune 500 companies building million-dollar sites who had high expectations their sites would be robust. We developed pre-defined reports to provide an understanding of how a business was doing online. These reports provided clues as to the changes needed to improve each visitor's journey.

The company had a superb story to tell.

It had created unprecedented insight and functionality. Benefits that higher end customers sorely needed to do big business online. This would be the basis for its own category. If we could successfully carve out that market niche, we had the potential to make this product a market leader.

Best of all, we offered a product that gave our customers needed insight. No other competitors offered such a solution. Ours directly scratched our customers' "itch."

The offering was extremely well received in analyst briefings when we launched. Press coverage was superb. We moved out of the unheated, unfurnished warehouse and into a proper office.

The company was on its way.

In July 1997, *Fortune* magazine recognized us as one of the "Top 25 Cool Companies" in Silicon Valley. The company successfully completed its IPO on NASDAQ in July 1999.

When to Create a New Market Category

Sometimes creating a new market category is the obvious way to go. You have your sights set on a particular market, but the existing categories don't suit you.

This may be the case if, and when, your unique competitive advantage is strong and distinctive: it sets you apart from your nearest competitors in ways that are *important* to the customer.

Creating a market category doesn't mean that you have no competitors. Your customer *always* has other options. Therefore, there are always other solutions the customer might choose.

You have competitors, and that's a good thing. You *want* competitors.

Competition validates that there's a market for what you're offering. You must get this confirmation before you attempt to create a new category, so you don't invest in creation of said category only to find out that no one cares!

Competition gives your customers a frame of reference to think about and compare your solution.

Competition provides the opportunity to communicate why your product is superior. That requires a reference point in your customer's mind.

In this example, Roberto's offering gave customers new insight into very important aspects of buyer behavior. This allowed people running online businesses to leapfrog forward.

It wasn't merely a better way to gather log file data; it was a better way to understand and guide the customer journey through the products and services they offered.

THE PATH TO REVENUE

You may have an innovative offering that involves either a breakthrough product or a breakthrough business model, or both.

In either case, if the customer is at the center of that product or model, it may be time to order a case of bubbly.

Advantages of Creating a New Market Category

Creating a new market category is not a simple task, it involves a great deal of market research and competitive intelligence—not to mention some serious PR. Doing so can also be worthwhile:

1. It can be lucrative!

Fortune examined the 100 fastest-growing U.S. companies from 2009–2011.[3] They discovered that over those three years, *the thirteen companies that had created their own categories* accounted for:

- 53 percent of incremental revenue growth
- 74 percent of incremental market capitalization growth

The message is simple: category creators experience much faster growth and receive much higher valuations from investors than companies bringing only incremental innovations to market.

2. You Gain Competitive Advantage

Give customers a reason to buy from you. It's not only the innovation that people will purchase; the accessories and complementary products often yield even greater revenues.

Best Buy created and launched Geek Squad—an installation, troubleshooting, and in-home service. The Geek Squad gave them a leg up when the business faced competition from low-priced online retailers.

And it made geeks across the nation feel better about themselves.

Just like the purchase of a car requires the ongoing refilling of the gas tank, owners of Keurig coffeemakers must buy single-serving coffee pods. The Keurig company which created that market owns not only

89

the original coffeemaker sales, but also the market for all the accessories—at least initially.

The company earned over $800 million in coffeemaker sales but another $3+ *billion* in pods. By creating the need for coffee in pods, Keurig created a temporary moat around their product. For the longest time, competing coffee beans weren't available in pods; customer had to buy their coffee refills from Keurig.

There are many other examples of well-known products that created new markets. Apple launched the iPod portable media player, then followed it with the launch of iTunes content. Sales of iPods peaked years ago, accounting for only 1.18% of Apple's total global revenue in 2018.[4] But Apple earns multiple *billions* in sales revenue of iPod accessories and products in the iTunes store.

3. You Control the Agenda

If you create the market, you get to state the criteria for success and to choose the yardstick by which to measure effectiveness, progress, or other variables.

- **Functionality:** Video game players that enabled people to play in teams or remotely against randomly assigned opponents, raised the bar on the simpler, original video game models.
- **Distribution:** DVD rental stores provided movie access for at-home viewing. Streaming changed all that and allowed Netflix to make former market boss Blockbuster say Uncle.

If you can offer a product or service that provides a better customer experience, you can control the agenda and you may define an entirely new market.

It's time to be creative.

THE PATH TO REVENUE

Tech Trends + Customer Need = New Markets

The internet changed how people live, work, play, and learn. When access became widely available and almost everyone was surfing the web, it was only a matter of time before curious teens started pushing the limits.

That gave rise to a spate of consumer software products intended to protect children by blocking nefarious web sites. The idea was to keep kids safe online and restrict their access to porn sites, violence, hate speech, and other sordid content which is better left to... well, their parents.

Buying and installing a filtering program gave parents some peace of mind.

The need to keep Johnny and Susie safe online formed a multi-million-dollar market; software packages retailed between $15 and $49 per user. Several vendors earned a slice of that market, spurred on by timely press coverage about the perils of the Internet and the need to keep children safe online.

As Internet access became more common at work, companies observed more employees going online to shop, date, house-hunt, job search, view porn, and many other activities deemed inappropriate.

Unhappy employers chafed at the excessive use of the high speed Internet access they provided for non-business purposes.

Experts lauded the recognized leader in consumer web filtering of inappropriate web content and keeping kids safe online. No one had been talking about using these filters in the office.

But there is always an opportunist looking for a void in a market.

Filling the Void

Matthew Smith was a good-natured and confident general manager of a leading consumer web filtering company. And he was very good at asking questions instead of making assumptions.

He called me after observing the work I had done in website analysis.

That company had defined the *high-end* market—then claimed and dominated it like a Golden Retriever does a toy. Matthew wanted to offer web content filtering in the workplace. It was an entirely fresh idea.

"What do you think, Theresa?"

Together ,we developed a strategy to adapt our technology for an entirely different purpose and to appeal to an entirely original audience.

That kind of new product launch—into a market that *we would create*—was enticing. I was soon on board with Smith to lead his marketing—charged with not only growing the consumer-filtering business, but building a business around the workplace product.

We outlined the potentially negative workplace issues and identified three major concerns:

- **Liability** stemming from a "hostile work environment" that could result when people use the office web for porn
- **Lost productivity** when workers spend a big chunk of their time online but not working
- **Bandwidth constraints** when inappropriate video streaming creates a bottleneck

These were the consequences of recreational surfing at work. But that was not enough to create a new market category. First, we needed to make the case for *addressing* these issues by quantifying the problem. Keep in mind that thought leadership is a strategic and legitimate means of creating an identity and it's indispensable when you want to create a new market category.

Thought Leadership in the Press

It helps to have the press on your side, so I chose to partner with Newsweek to help create this new market. According to *Newsweek*:

THE PATH TO REVENUE

"A new generation of cyber slacking workers are multi-shirking by spending hours a day frittering away time online. As e-mail and high-speed internet access have become standard-issue office equipment, rampant abuse of computers in the workplace is making the water cooler look like a font of productivity. For bosses, cyber slacking is becoming a pervasive and perplexing problem in the new wired workplace."[5]

This kind of well-placed, thought-leadership article can be tremendously useful in an effort to create a new market.

Next, I developed a PR campaign that assigned some rather revealing numbers to these issues. The goal was to promote the concept ahead of the offering, like the aroma from a kitchen teases the upcoming meal.

I created several press releases announcing our findings in each of these three workplace areas. We were highlighting a problem to which we were about to offer a solution.

Newsweek wrote:

"Corporations are scrambling to measure the problem. According to a recent survey by Vault.com, 90 percent of the nation's workers admit to surfing recreational sites during office hours. And 84 percent of workers say they send personal e-mail from work. American workers spend [an estimated] one-third of their time on the net; cheating the boss out of actual work, double last year's rate of on-the-job, recreational surfing."[6]

To tailor the product offering for corporate use, we added prepackaged reports for both IT and line managers, and a robust admin interface for the IT department.

Finally, we needed a catchy name for our offering to help people "get" it right away. Eventually, we rolled out our '@Work' offering.

An excellent review in a prominent publication helped solidify the creation of the market and our dominance:

"Sporting the smoothest, most intuitive interface of any product we reviewed, [this product] is an administrator's dream.... did a good job filtering material right out of the box; solid reporting and management flexibility make it the best overall solution for creating an intelligent internet policy."

We had successfully created a large niche for ourselves. As the only player in that niche market at the time, we were the dominant offering.

Category is Important!

A market category is a frame of reference for your customers. People need that to understand and really "get" your brand. Having a frame of reference helps people think about a category of solutions and yours in particular.

Sometimes, your market category is not serving your brand, and you need to forge a new category.

Creating a new market category is difficult, but can be an ingenious way to position your brand for success. It's also one of the best ways to achieve market dominance.

For many companies, developing consistent and interesting messaging is hard enough. However, the rewards of creating a new category can be great. Category creators often experience much faster growth and higher valuations from investors than companies who bring only incremental innovations to market.

Practical customers in mainstream markets prefer to buy from market leaders. Lest you think market category creation is a thing of the past, here are a few of the numerous companies that have done this successfully in the last decade, and now are household names:

- **Airbnb**–residential hospitality,
- **NetSuite**–cloud-based business management systems,
- **Peloton**–indoor cycling,
- **Quicken**–personal financial management software,
- **Quora**–a Q&A platform to gain knowledge,
- **ServiceNow**–employee workflow platform,
- **Slack Technologies**–a proprietary instant messaging platform,
- **Stripe**–payments software,

THE PATH TO REVENUE

- **Venmo**—send and receive payments direct to checking accounts,

All of these companies created their own market category. They each carved out their own market niche.

You'll notice that many of these companies are subscription models. Many have a hardware component combined with a software or service subscription.

Consider leveraging a SaaS business model. Delivering software as a subscription service usually involves lower start-up costs for the vendor and lower entry fees for the customer. It also forms a relationship with the customer from the beginning which builds loyalty, makes revenue streams more predictable, and makes repeat business more likely.

The brilliance of SaaS is that it makes your offering "sticky" by design.

Customers sign up for your service, because they believe they have an ongoing need. If you work hard at delighting your customer, you have a model that will keep them coming back.

Even if your product is not a subscription model, it pays to have a plan for retaining customers. What you will offer them in the future? How will you keep them satisfied?

Creating a new market category is a difficult undertaking requiring enormous effort—yet it is one of the most strategic initiatives a B2B company can undertake.

The company will substantially improve its chances of success.

Which can also be extremely lucrative.

APPLICATION

1. Let your imagination run wild! Give yourself permission to think creatively.

2. Be very clear about why category creation is an outstanding idea—both for your company and for the customer.

3. Don't let the magnitude of the idea intimidate you. If market conditions point to new category creation as a wise strategy, create it!

4. Lay the groundwork. Set the stage while the solution or product is in development. Get customer input along the way.

5. Embrace and acknowledge your competition. They are the pillars that give your market position power and stability. Remember that positioning is competitive by definition.

6. Make it sticky. Start from the beginning with an approach that builds ongoing demand—and have a roadmap to meet that demand. This will help you to maintain your dominant position as category leader and "king" of the category you just created.

7. Be intentional about your selected business model. Consider whether a SaaS business is applicable for the category you create.

8. Be careful in product design. Work with engineering to strike the right balance. When considering the new product or service, does the customer need to take small steps that are different or can the customer handle a monumental change in how this need is met? (Reference the technology adoption discussion in Ch.3).

9. Look for opportunities to sell accessories or complementary products and services. For example, smartphone accessory products include protective hard covers, plastic screen protectors, ear buds, chargers, power cables, and adapters. These add-ons can easily add up to more revenue than the original core product.

FINAL THOUGHTS

Market creation is not about doing something slightly different or better than the others. It means creating a market that did not exist before.

The rewards are plentiful.

Few growth strategies match the economics of category creation.[1] Time after time, consumers reward new category companies with both revenue growth and stock price appreciation.

Creating a new category of market demand does not guarantee you will dominate over the long haul.

Ask Myspace. Myspace was similar to, but preceded Facebook and, for a time from 2005 to 2008 was the largest social media site in the world.[2] (Raise your hand if you've ever heard of them before).

However, every competitor that enters after you just helps the size of the overall market grow.

There's wisdom in the old saying, "A rising tide lifts all boats." Practical customers in mainstream markets prefer to buy from market leaders. Creating your own category is one of the best ways to achieve market dominance.

Just remember to remain *customer-centric* and not *customer-driven*.

Creating and growing a new market can be lucrative, as Roberto's company discovered. What if your company tries to grow in a different way, internationally? Read on to find out exactly when the time is right to go global.

7

BEING SAVVY ABOUT CHANNEL GROWTH

> Be International or Fail." –William H. Davidow, Author of *Marketing High Technology*

Camille was an enchanting, chic, and cheerful woman straight out of Paris. She was one of the three French co-founders of a technical software company and head of international business.

The company made software development tools (software for building software)—high tech just doesn't get any 'techier' than that! The US side of the business was going well. Gross margins on software are high, and about half of total company revenue was generated in the US, with the other half came from the direct offices in France and Japan.

While Camille worked daily with the team in Paris, she had only one person in her group devoted to building international sales. Margaret was that jack-of-all-trades with huge responsibilities—sales quotas, channel marketing, recruitment, onboarding, and revenue growth.

Camille knew that the profitable domestic business had tremendous potential in markets outside the US.

Their offering allowed developers to create cross-platform apps that work on a variety of operating systems and languages. This unique ability to localize was important for international expansion.

So global growth potential was promising, but Camille's company needed some kind of order and focus to grow international channels successfully.

Serving Customer Needs Globally

Camille met me with her standard "Bonjour!" greeting, which always made me crave a chocolate croissant.

We talked at length about her company and its products, the state of the market, and the revenue she hoped to soon realize. While domestic revenues were growing at a rate over 20 percent annually, Camille wanted to *double* company revenues through a concentrated focus on international expansion.

"But, where to start?" she wondered out loud. "How do we go about this?"

I told her it wouldn't be easy. "But we can get there with planning and research. We need to set in motion a systematic, measured plan to develop our international channels," I explained.

"We'll establish a repeatable process for partner selection and recruitment, partner onboarding, and revenue growth. We need a partner program with an ordered, structured focus."

"First, we prioritize our markets. Right now we don't know whether Australia or England has greater potential, or whether Hong Kong or Germany is the larger market. We need to decide where there's the most potential—based on the total available market in each country. Then we'll rank order our target countries."

I laid out a six-month plan for Camille that began with market research and then called for selecting, recruiting, and onboarding a whole new set of capable partners. We would need to travel to get to know these folks, understand their business, train, and coach them to be successful with our product line. "Whatever you need!" she said.

Getting Set up for Success

Camille relied upon a savvy sales pro, Margaret, who had a great head for numbers and an instinct for opportunity. She was a huge asset at headquarters.

We hired a product expert, Scott, to talk technical specifics with potential partners. I would assess them from the business perspective, and Scott would train them on our solutions.

Scott could hold his own in any technical conversation. And his personality and sense of adventure made our global travels fun.

Traveling is great, but author Al Boliska once described the actual flying part this way:

"Airline travel is hours of boredom interrupted by moments of stark terror."

There's some truth to that, along with the myriad of other hassles that can arise, like TSA issues, flight delays and someone sitting near you that smells like a yak.

Pre-COVID I would have suggested that you buck up and deal with the inconveniences of long flights to visit your partners regularly. For now, things are very different and international travel is less practical; maybe even frowned upon. You can still honor the spirit of the idea: get your business partners and potential channel folks on a Zoom call whenever the need arises. Discuss the issues at hand, eye to eye. Don't let the misunderstandings and miscommunications pile up over time.

We looked for global partners who had a handle on the market and customers in each country. I could do much of that work from Palo Alto. Through initial phone calls, interviews, and industry research, we identified the partners who worked in our broad market category.

These potential partners had to know how to build a business, so we looked for proven success in other areas. They strove toward profitability and had to understand how to talk with and qualify customers.

I would identify the next country on our list and set up meetings with partner candidates in that country.

After we identified potential partners in our target markets, Scott and I hit the road. We met in person with every partner we were considering for our business. Involving top management of each company in the discussions was a requirement. We needed commitment from the top.

We asked them how they built their business, how they chose new product lines, how they qualified customers, and how they presented new opportunities. Scott and I spent two weeks in Europe, two weeks at home, two weeks in Asia, then two weeks at home.

We did this for the next four years.

Scott and I covered most of Europe and Asia—establishing our business in thirty countries. One by one we found partners who understood software development and wanted to offer our developer tools. As head of international marketing, I worked with a team to recruit, select, train, and support these reps all over the world.

We took great care to spend time and understand the new partners we brought into the family. We were such a small team we could not afford to make mistakes. . You'll save a lot of time these days, meeting by Zoom.

We decided that Scott, Margaret, and I would not invest time, effort, and money in partners who could not—or would not—be successful.

Recruitment was the most critical step. Because we hired the right partner, we found that our time onboarding, training, and coaching them led to revenue growth that exceeded our expectations.

I'll take that kind of surprise any day.

While the domestic business continued to grow at 20 percent annually, overall global company revenues *more* than doubled each year for the next four years, mainly through the new international channels.

THE PATH TO REVENUE

Be International or Fail

As I learned at Camille's company, overcoming obstacles and seizing opportunities are crucial when you venture into foreign markets. This applies to all types of businesses, not only tech companies.

Obstacles are plentiful and can arise out of nowhere like prairie dogs. These include:

- The amount of concentrated effort involved in establishing new channels
- Required product modifications
- Generating new documentation to support those product modifications
- Internationalization of the product as well as the documentation
- Navigating the import/export regulations
- Not being able to dictate the same terms for business overseas

The *opportunities,* however, can be extremely worthwhile.

Every point of global market share makes you a stronger competitor at home and adds to your bottom line. Plus, exposure to more competitors will also strengthen your organization. Finally, geographic diversification decreases risk in the big picture of your corporate portfolio.

Additional stability is an advantage, too. Not to mention the added revenue.

If you win in the global market, you win at home, and that reinforces itself.

Assuming that your eventual goal is to dominate the market, you can't limit your view of "your market" to the domestic market. You may face foreign competitors here at home. The best defense is a good offense.

When you're ready to expand geographically, you may be ready to go international. It's something to consider, even for smallish companies.

Customer-Centric International Channels

So the question should be *when* are you ready to tackle international expansion? Not if, but when.

Some companies grapple with this for months or years and have a tough time answering it. Is it when revenues in the US hit a particular level? When you've earned a certain size market share? When you hit a certain number of employees?

The time to expand internationally is when you've bullet-proofed your business model. A proven business model that's running smoothly may very well be ready for international expansion.

That doesn't mean you have to establish a presence with direct sales offices in multiple countries. For most young companies, partnering is the smartest path.

Look at building revenue through international channel partners as a process comprising *three steps*: partner selection, partner onboarding, and growth.

First: Partner Selection and Recruitment.

As is true in skydiving, the first step is the most important one. Your choice of partners determines where, and in whom, you invest your time, travel, and effort.

Be careful not to select partners just because they have all the right logos on their website. Doing so is like marrying someone because you like their tattoos.

Try to divine if they truly understand your business. Ask yourself, "What's in it for them?" Yes, you want them to be motivated to make money, but you need to go deeper.

Understand their history, how they make money, how they're positioned in the market, and how they're perceived by their customers. Understand why they want to work with you.

THE PATH TO REVENUE

Know where their motivation comes from and how they plan to succeed. Your future partner must know the local competitive landscape, customers, and solution—then they'll be able to introduce your solution into that market effectively.

You also want to be sure that your new partners are committed to running a "customer-centric" business. You want them to stay in business for a long time and have a great future in front of them. You both want to remain partners on the long 'path to revenue' and be successful together.

Second: Partner Onboarding.

You've selected each partner because you know they have the "recipe" to grow successfully. Now coach them how to apply that recipe to *your* business.

Make it easy for them to do that through training, coaching, and explaining your market positioning. Share your best tips and questions to qualify customers so your partner has insight into why customers choose your solutions.

They'll soon sell as effectively as you do. Ideally, you want to ensure that your partner is making money in the first 120 days.

Within twelve to eighteen months, a new partner should perform at target revenue rates. Nurture partners who have their eye on the prize and are working to include your insight into their ongoing business.

Third: Growth.

Third, the ongoing coaching relationship established with each partner enables you to take your business to the next level together.

You can motivate first-graders with rewards like recess and cupcakes, but the North Star of the business world is corporate profit and compensation. Set up a bonus system that rewards the stars in your channel program. Encourage them to focus on the partners who are doing well now or have the potential to do so, based on their full pipeline.

Similar to the star employees on your own team, compensate partner reps for their wins, and be clear about what they need to do to earn the next level reward. Partners should be able to reference a formal, written program and know how much money they'll make selling each product at each revenue level.

Growing Channels in Asia

Stuart Franks was a wise, magnanimous VP of marketing. He oversaw global growth of an expansive line of network security solutions. The domestic business was robust despite a plethora of competitors.

Stuart's charter there was to grow the business at a healthy rate that exceeded market expansion. Internationally, the company had a loose collection of disparate channel partners that met with varied levels of success.

Ninety-five countries make up the Asia-Pacific region. In some countries, managers led fully staffed offices of sales, marketing and technical support.

In other countries, managers ran their own offices but had fewer resources to serve the vast, local business. In even smaller markets, country managers were responsible for revenue goals, but there was no formal office presence to support them. Each setup was different.

These in-country leaders had quarterly revenue goals to meet. Some felt isolated from corporate headquarters by the long distance. The lack of consistent communication and support from Corporate was a challenge for many.

When I met Stuart, he spoke respectfully about everyone in the company and complimented his team on the superb work they were doing. Then he explained the situation.

"Theresa, our team in Asia needs attention. We need to both communicate better and to support them more effectively. We are doing excel-

THE PATH TO REVENUE

lent marketing here, and we need to leverage that to help grow international revenues.

"We have mostly the right partners, but they need more coaching in our way of doing business. Most Americans, by nature, concentrate on the US business. We need someone on our team who will live and breathe for the Asia-Pacific region at Corporate. It's a vast territory, including a myriad of countries and cultures, and they need a champion at Corporate."

I saw what he was talking about. A robust, detailed US newsletter went to American partners each week. How could we do that across Asia? How could we get the word out about quarterly promotions? Would a newsletter work in Asia? Would the same promotions work in Asia?

Was there marketing content that might be helpful in China, Australia, and across the Pacific Rim countries? How could we leverage competitive intelligence to fight the competition effectively?

Should we replicate the annual partner conference held in the US in Asia? What could translate from one country to another, or from one culture to another? What would not?

"The one thing that's carved in stone," Stuart noted, "is that we are a purely channel organization. One-hundred percent of our business goes through the channel, not just smaller deals. The job of our sales team is to support the channel partner and help them close business. The channel partner—our representative in each country—is the customer of our sales team. We need to maintain our commitment to the channel above all else."

I suggested that we start with a combination approach. It would combine his company's tried-and-true recipe for success with the flexibility needed to adapt on the fly.

We would work with marketing managers to implement our marketing programs in-country, asking for feedback from the teams at every step.

We'd be available to share 'best practices' from the U.S. and work together to adapt them so they would work well in all the countries in our territory. Using some existing programs was acceptable. We tweaked them to suit each country. The focus was on communicating value—such as best practices from California—and letting the Asian country managers determine what would and what would not work in their own markets.

My role was to provide both information and support. If we had the right partners on our team, the job was to enable them through information and resources. I had regular conversations with the country managers and partners who were successful. If they said they needed something—be it providing competitive intel or arranging a press conference—I was on it. They knew their business and what they needed, and I made sure they got it.

If the Indian and Japanese resellers *both* needed their own dedicated conference at a resort, okay! We flew eighty resellers from each country to Macau for back-to-back conferences in the same hotel. Doing so ensured I could get the most from the hotel's event-planning staff and also maximize the time invested by people who flew in from California.

Speaking of global opportunities, if ever you end up in Macau, you'll find the highest bungy jump in the world. Note to self: never dare an Indian reseller sitting next to you on the tour bus by saying, "I will if you will." He'll take you up on it. Then you *have to* follow through or lose face. It was the *most terrifying* minute of my life. Lesson learned.

If the Southeast Asia resellers were happy to mix with the partners from Australia and New Zealand, okay! We flew them to Kuala Lumpur for three days of meetings. Everyone was happy to meet the product managers from California.

We tailored the entertainment and activities to delight teams from each culture so they could enjoy themselves like kids whacking a piñata.

At each of these conferences, our partners received all corporate news before we made it public. They could plan their own press conferences and announce their own news. We gained points with them as we kept them in the know.

We developed and implemented our efforts regarding the channel partners and the businesses they were running. If we had been selecting brand new partners, it would have made more sense to *tell them* how things run in our business.

But, like a parent who needs to shift from director to coach as their child grows up, we had to be more flexible. We could offer experience and lessons learned, but we couldn't force these on our country managers or partners. In the big picture, we developed overall sales and marketing channel strategies to be in line with corporate positioning, and we were on hand to support the implementation of tactics in-country, as needed.

The results were obvious. In two years, we doubled market share and revenues for our network security solutions in Asia Pacific. In addition, WiPro/India recognized my client as the "Vendor with Best Marketing" and ZDNet/Asia named us one of the Top Ten Fastest Growing Private Companies in Asia.

Recognized as a serious vendor in network security solution, we rose in those markets and became the leader in the Asia-Pacific market.

Customer-Centric Best Practices

It's important to keep on top of sales reports to ensure that you know who your top partners are. Then treat them as such. Maintain constant communication with them as you would when your teenage wild-child is out on a Saturday night.

Industry-wide, two percent of the partners generate roughly 40 percent of profitable revenue.[1] Each partner could represent a significant investment of our time and budget, so it makes good sense to invest heavily and intentionally in the top performers, or those with the potential to join that two percent.

At any point, you can do a mental check of your current partners. Research the partner company to find out what they are trying to achieve. Are their clients matching up with yours? Are their goals aligned with yours? Do they have the skill set needed for a successful implementation?

When considering who might be an ideal channel partner, ask these questions:[2]

- **Are they ready?** Do they have the resources to invest in the partnership?
- **Are they willing?** Will the partnership help them reach their goals?
- **Are they able?** Is there a technical fit? A competence fit?
- **Do we have similar values?** Is there a culture fit?
- **Do they have a "customer-centric" mindset?**
- **Do they smell like a yak?**

If the answer to the first five questions is *yes*, you are on the right path. Overlooking the last one just might be worthwhile.

If the potential partner's key objectives align with your direction, then the partnership might very well help you both achieve your goals. If that's the case, double down on coaching, training, and marketing assistance.

Support your partners with quarterly promotions and matched marketing dollars. Work with them to get to the next tier of the partner program. If the times allow, schedule a corporate visit to their territory; meet some customers and hold a press conference while you're there. If not, do what you can via video chat. Ask them what else would help boost sales.

APPLICATION

1. Prioritize your target market countries; know why country #1 is at the top of your list.

2. Do not rush or take shortcuts in partner selection and recruitment. This is *the* most important step in your process. Choose and invest in partners with both the ability and motivation to be highly successful.

3. Involve the most senior level of management to ensure they are committed to making the partnership successful.

4. Ask a lot of questions about their business before you both commit. If possible, go on sales calls with the partner and watch them in action.

5. Spend time with new partners by onboarding and training them in person or through Zoom. Don't simply share your positioning in the competitive landscape, explain *why* it is the way it is. Reveal all your very best tips for customer engagement and qualification—don't hold back any information that might help them learn how to best present your solutions.

6. Facilitate their growth to help them meet revenue rate goals. Spend time in-country to share your best marketing strategies, competitive insights, and new product news. Use PR to build awareness and generate demand to build a successful presence in that country. Work with them.

7. Evaluate performance regularly. If they're not on target within 18 months, identify and address the issues. Set a meeting to review the reasons for falling short.

8. Incentivize and reward for growth with a solid, transparent, consistent compensation plan.

FINAL THOUGHTS

A rich network of motivated, well-chosen channel partners who are treated like valued customers yields significant benefits:

- Faster growth for the global corporation
- Greater awareness about your company
- Larger market share
- Increased revenue to your bottom line
- Brand presence in new markets

Selecting the right partners is the key to efficient, faster international growth. It also requires substantial thought, in-person discussion, and research up front to ensure that you are selecting the right partners. Onboard them efficiently, and support them as much as possible to help them grow.

Taking your business on a global journey requires a clear vision of the process involved. What if your customers cannot see which of your product offerings best suits them? Turn the page to find out how one client dealt with that very problem, solved it and found their way to success.

Just like you can.

8

DIFFERENTIATE TO STAND OUT

> "Slightly better is dangerous."
>
> — William H. Davidow, *Marketing High Technology*

Imagine seeing two desserts listed on a restaurant menu, with two different prices, but no description of the difference between them. You know you want dessert, but how to decide?

In the business world, a company must differentiate their product offerings from one another so customers can best choose which one suits their needs. If there is any confusion, customers will move on to a competitor who presents their solutions more clearly.

Bruno led marketing for a respected major maker of capital equipment for the semiconductor industry—a company with a strong reputation for innovation.

They enjoyed several years of success selling their first product line. When Bruno's product team announced a second line of equipment, the company had two distinct and separately branded products for one process.

But customers were confused about which system to choose; both did basically the same process. When both product lines were side-by-side on the pricing sheet, the difference in cost showed the customer that the newer system was 'better:' one cost ~$500K and the other over $1 million.

The company was differentiating on price alone.

The sales team got no direction about when to sell which product. The head of product marketing, Joe, knew they could do a better job of presenting their product line benefits. Doing so would differentiate between the two lines and help them stand above the competition.

If differences were better articulated, that would help the sales team present their solutions more clearly. It would empower the sales reps to guide their prospects to the best choice of product to meet their specific needs.

Establishing a Customer-Centric Plan

They hired me to lead the marketing communications efforts, and I dug in to address these challenges with the product management team. We agreed that each person involved in the sale should be able to articulate the benefits of each system and then recommend the solution that best met the customer needs.

Marketing communications for highly technical product lines is like being an interpreter: it was my job to clearly translate technical jargon into attributes and customer benefits.

We assessed all the competitive products on the market and developed an objective matrix that included a side-by-side comparison of our product line with those of our competitors. Working closely with the product team, we developed messaging tailored for each of our products.

When we reviewed feature comparisons and messaging for the two product lines, it was clear that we were getting in our own way. The two products were competing against each other.

That was an enormous problem!

So we figured out what we did better than the competition. This was the ammunition—the reasons customers would buy our system instead of the competition.

We enumerated half a dozen ways we beat out the others. We defined the key benefits of each of our two solutions, then aligned them to customer needs. We also had a decision-making guide that gave people the information they needed to evaluate similar product lines.

Finally the differentiation was clear.

Product or service differentiation is the introduction of distinctive characteristics or features to a product or service to ensure a USP (unique selling proposition). The differentiation allows a company to achieve a competitive advantage over, or stand out from, other companies offering similar products. It is an essential marketing process that is of vital economic importance to a business. [1]

Differentiate with a Customer-Centric Perspective

We viewed it like a decision tree: the answer to each question determined the next question.

Example.

A semiconductor fab manager would evaluate etch equipment first by type (dry vs. wet etching), then by etch material (chemical or ionized gas), and, finally, by film type. That narrowed down the brands to be evaluated.

Once we knew which products were contenders, we could base a deeper evaluation on specific etch criteria:

- Performance (measured in nanometers)
- Throughput (# wafers/hour)
- Conductivity (accuracy)
- Defect rates (contamination)

This would determine the customer's choice of machine—now they knew which product to select to meet their needs. Doing this exercise for each product led us to uncover the true strengths—the ability to etch multi-layer film stacks with extreme selectivity at a low overall cost per wafer.

We were demonstrably better at that than any other vendor.

Presenting clear details about our product performance empowered our sales team to satisfy our customers' needs. One line was best suited to customers making high density, low cost memory chip; the other was best suited for special application, more expensive custom circuits.

Others Involved In The Purchase

In a technical sale like this, the capital equipment price tags range from $1 million to $3 million per system. With a financial outlay of this size, the purchase approval on the customer side involves not only the fab manager, but also several other technical people and members of the executive team, including the CFO, and possibly even the CEO.

We needed to present our competitive positioning and product attributes clearly to non-technical customers who might influence the purchase decision.

This was imperative.

(For more on that, reference the discussion on empowering Sales with customer-centric content in Ch.5.)

Ammunition for Sales

My team dug in and created "sell kits" for each of the product lines. Each sell kit showed the process, the material and film types used, and the key applications for which it was best suited.

Next, we indicated how our system performed with respect to a lengthy list of material and process-dependent criteria. Finally, we offered a total cost of ownership analysis using theoretical numbers to give customers the ability to estimate fab costs in a production environment.

We could back up our claim that these state-of-the-art etch products were best at providing exceptional uniformity, selectivity, and productivity with the lowest defects.

Eventually, we did the same for the rest of the product lines, identifying the most outstanding attributes of each product. We evaluated using the same approach our customers would use to decide which brands they would consider. This customer-centric approach served the sales team well.

As a result, we grew market share from single digits to 27% in two years. Revenue grew at an equally impressive rate and the company became known as a major player in the industry. It still is today. (And I'm still kicking myself for selling that stock!).

Product Advantages Pave The Way For Brand Building

Products such as laptops, iPhones, PCs, and cameras get smaller yet more powerful every year. The performance challenge for chip makers is staying a step ahead of the evolution by providing ever-smaller and denser chip features.

Chips get smaller and wafers get bigger so there are more devices on—and more investment in—each wafer. For this reason, today's leading-edge equipment won't suffice in five years. Advanced techniques enable chip makers to deliver increasingly powerful devices and leading-edge solutions across their broadening product line.

Differentiation

Differentiation is one of the core principles of marketing theory and practice. Strong, successful differentiation helps you stand out from your competition and is useful to your company in the following ways:

- It gives your sales people ammunition, so they can be successful in giving your customer reasons to select your product,
- It empowers your marketing efforts with an interesting message foundation for successful campaigns
- It unveils insight for your product management and engineering teams to carve out the future roadmap

Two Kinds of Differentiation

There are two ways you can approach differentiation—you can focus on differentiating your products and services, or differentiating your company brand to rise above your competitors' brands.

Product differentiation serves as a catalyst in the purchase decision-making process. It sets one product apart from the rest and serves as the deciding factor in purchase decisions.[2]

Differentiate your product by highlighting size, packaging, features, ingredients, origin, functionality or a myriad of other product attributes.

Corporate, or brand name differentiation, on the other hand, can allow for a variety of novel approaches. For example:

- A focus on customer service, or a goal to define and deliver a world-class customer experience (i.e., Crystal Cruises)
- A unique distribution channel or method, (DoorDash)
- The relationship with your partners (or customers) to deliver unprecedented value or convenience (Wells Fargo branches inside of Safeway stores)
- Image and reputation differentiation (Tiffany & Co.)

Any of these approaches to brand differentiation can be very compelling.

In addition, especially with consumer products, there may be several brands housed under one corporate name. Just look at Procter &

Gamble or Johnson & Johnson. To keep things simple, however, most smaller companies—those who are concerned about not being among the 9 in 10 that fail—start out as one-product companies. One product brands.

For the capital equipment maker, a focused effort on brand building paid off in accelerated growth rate. In two years, revenues tripled and market share grew from 19% to 27%, according to VLSI Research, who tracked the industry at the time.

We also enjoyed huge gains in brand awareness and propensity to buy, as measured by VLSI. We based the brand reputation on the pillars of innovation and precision, which continues to serve the company well.

Today the company is short-listed on nearly every new fab's vendor list as they evaluate and specify equipment purchases.

The Crowded Field of Enterprise Software

While Bruno and his team had to differentiate between their in-house offerings, Miguel Lopez, CEO of an enterprise software solutions company, faced the challenge of differentiating his company from the competition.

Miguel was pleased his business had earned a very positive reputation across Europe. The Spanish company had grown market share for its innovative application performance management (APM) solutions, working with customers in Spain, Italy, Germany, Belgium and the UK.

Then they set their sights on the US market. Miguel did not underestimate the challenge of getting visibility among the myriad of competitors: he knew that the US market was vast and highly competitive. He knew he would need an effective strategy to stand out and earn market share.

Always Focus on the Customer

Miguel hired me to manage the US market launch and he briefed me on his company's offering. "Standing out in a crowded field would be a test of the company's strength," he shared. "It means stepping up our game and presenting a more polished brand to the larger US enterprise market." We needed both a launch strategy and clear, compelling messaging.

The competitive landscape of the American market consisted of enormous companies, such as CA, IBM, HP, and Compuware, among others.

All of them had software solutions they called "application performance management" or "application performance monitoring," that did more reporting than diagnosing.

What Miguel's company had uncovered, however, was another important capability.

While managing IT infrastructure in an application-centric manner, the key to thwarting obstacles is the ability to not just identify and diagnose problems, but to also repair them quickly. This repair capability is what would fuel the application performance management software market growth over the coming decade.

That was their key to differentiation.

The initial offering featured a tool capable of diagnosing performance issues in a simple and effective way.

The tool automatically, and nearly instantly, managed and diagnosed problems in our clients' IT platforms. This enabled the tool to not only point out any problem but to also *identify its root cause* in the first minute.[3]

It accomplished all of this with the unprecedented simplicity of a PB&J sandwich.

Our research into the American market showed that the challenge of diagnosing and repairing problems was a prime concern and an unmet need here, too, in spite of the large number of giant competitors. Even though it was only one of our many product attributes, we put it front and center because it was most important to our customer.

With that powerful product advantage and distinct differentiation, we successfully launched into the US market, praised by press and industry analysts.

In September 2012, Gartner recognized us as one of their *"Cool Vendors of* 2012," a high honor.

According to Gartner, we had set the bar for managing and optimizing application performance with such key benefits as code-level diagnostics, self-learning, and predictive performance analytics.

Getting a good reception in the market was important to solidify the brand and make it an attractive acquisition. CEO Miguel was extremely pleased with this lucrative acquisition. "With Theresa's crucial guidance, our company was successfully acquired", he said.

Our marketing strategy was to differentiate the product based on functional capabilities that customers were demanding.

They found the messaging to be interesting and valuable. The marketing focus on diagnostics was an effective difference-maker. The company continued on a path to accelerated revenues for its new parent company.

We discussed positioning in this book prior to differentiation for good reason.

Good positioning gives your target customer context, as if to say, "Here's the ball game we're playing and here are the ground rules."

When your customer has context, they can then compare your solution to others in the same category. This is great news because now you can set the agenda—you give them a yardstick to measure your offering and that of your competition.

This defines the big picture and, inside of that, we can see how everyone measures up.

Strong *product* differentiation enables the seller to contrast their product with competing products on the market and emphasize the unique aspects that make their product superior.

It helps you compete effectively because it enables you to stand out and get noticed for an attribute at which you excel that is important to your customers.

Strong *brand* differentiation can empower you to defend a premium price, while also serving as a basis to charge a top price for your *product*.

A higher price also helps establish perceived value in the customer's eyes—every white Starbuck's cup carried into any office anywhere is proof of this.

It also helps you to compete in areas *other than* price. This is important since competing on price is one of the weakest possible positions.

You don't want to win a deal only because your solution is the cheapest! It's better to win a deal because your solution best meets your customers' need.

Differentiation based on company name or brand is also successful when it builds loyalty.

Customers tend to choose a name brand or a company to which they feel loyal. Customer loyalty is one of Trader Joe's greatest strengths. Companies like Best Western, Marriott Hotels and American Airlines have strong frequent traveler programs that reward customer loyalty.

Differentiating well is essential. It allows the seller to contrast its own product with competing products in the market and emphasize the unique aspects that make its product superior.[4] Overall, differentiation allows a company to achieve a competitive advantage over other companies offering similar products or product substitutes.

It is an essential marketing process that is of vital economic importance to a business.[5] Good brand differentiation requires a 'customer-centric mindset.'

APPLICATION

Being intentional about your points of differentiation, and taking a customer-centric approach, is vital.

1. Analyze the industry and study the competition to get a clear picture of their strengths and weaknesses compared to your own.

2. Determine if your approach should begin with company/brand differentiation or product/service differentiation.

3. Read customers' reviews of your competitors. Note what strengths and weaknesses they highlight.

4. Base the differentiation on the attribute(s) considered most important by the customer, especially if this gives you a competitive advantage. Then, identify the areas in which you outshine the competition.

5. Before carving your "point of differentiation" message(s) in stone, test it.

Test it on customers. See if it resonates. See if your customers consider these areas to be of key importance. If so, test it on analyst groups. See if it resonates. Listen to the feedback from both customers and analysts. They know the market. Testing and gathering feedback will give you a strong indication whether this messaging will be successful, or if you haven't quite nailed it yet. In that case, you'll need to change it.

6. Once you're locked in, reinforce your differentiation in all your messaging. Be consistent as you hammer home this differentiation in every piece of communications—all collateral, all copy, all social media.

FINAL THOUGHTS

Competition is a wonderful thing because it gives your customer a frame of reference. It points to the need to be intentional about how you stand out.

Don't leave your differentiation to chance, or your competition will define you. Differentiating your brand and your products is critically important. Do it through your product's unique value or through your brand strengths. Whether you choose the product or brand approach, be intentional about your differentiation strategy.

When you are ready to implement your differentiation, it will serve as the foundation of your messaging. Your top-level message carries the differentiation. It is further explained in the detailed messaging through supporting proof points—much like the sub-title of a book supports and explains the title.

Differentiation empowers the sales team to sell each product more efficiently and effectively. It's an essential marketing process that is of vital economic importance to a business.[1] Good brand differentiation requires a 'customer-centric mindset.

Providing clarity between the solutions you offer by differentiating products can save your business. Sometimes clarity between your business' sales and marketing is the answer. Chapter 9 tells the story of a client who needed this internal transparency to avoid joining the 90% of startups that fail.

9

ALIGNING SALES AND MARKETING

> When sales and marketing align, your company optimizes their marketing and sales cycles as a whole, resulting in reduced costs and an increase in growth. Sales and marketing alignment can lead to a 32 percent increase in year-over-year (YoY) revenue growth."
>
> —Aberdeen Group, 'Why Alignment Is Worth The Effort,' Feb. 2016[1]

What follows is a cautionary tale of why transparency between sales and marketing departments is vital.

As a VP of sales at a B2B SaaS company, Luke's task was to jump-start sales for a new business unit. I served as head of marketing at the company.

Luke liked to keep things close to the vest. He refused to share his sales pipeline with anyone but his own team. He had zero interest in coordinating marketing campaigns with his sales outreach. Worst of all, he would not share any customer feedback from his sales calls—or any information for that matter—with the marketing team.

Each time he returned from a trade show, the marketing team was eager to hear how it went.

"Good," he said.

"Uh, Luke, I'm looking for a bit more detail. Did the booth visitors answer our qualifying questions? What did they have to say about our new product? Any input on features? What about pricing? How did the competition look at this show? And, BTW, where is your stack of business cards?"

Crickets.

Without feedback, it was impossible to adjust our marketing efforts. Was that a good show for us? Did the messaging resonate? We don't know. Another marketing professional likened it to bowling in the dark, without lanes, without bumpers to guide you, hoping for a strike.

Hope is not a plan.

Fictional Customers = Real Losses

Eventually, under pressure to do so, Luke revealed his pipeline. There were leads he hadn't engaged with yet and some he'd already lost. Some he had never called upon. No wonder there was no feedback. No wonder Luke had closed so few deals!

There was absolutely no transparency in this situation. I couldn't see the pipeline and there was no record of conversations with prospects entered in our database. Without the ability to review the sales data and the customer input, marketing campaigns don't have the input needed to improve.

To become more customer-centric, the company felt that all departments had to work together. With no input from sales, one of the biggest antennae was missing. Luke left the company and, with a new sales team in place, we determined next steps.

Sales And Marketing: Necessary Partners

Together, we revisited our target customer profiles and lead qualification criteria. Then we analyzed the demand gen plans and programs for every stage of the sales funnel. The key word is *together.* When we started working *together*, everything clicked. Revenue soared.

This story has a happy ending. When sales and marketing share information, great things happen. The company eventually went public in a successful IPO.

> *"You must align sales and marketing if you want to navigate the path to revenue successfully."*

Sales and marketing can work together like a hand in glove, peas and carrots, or peanut butter and jelly. They just naturally go together. Or at least they *should* go together. If they don't, the big picture is incomplete, and results are thwarted.

Any early stage company whose sales and marketing executives don't get along, like, and respect each other, will encounter stalled growth. Or at least, that's my experience. They won't achieve anywhere what their potential *could* be. It's not a healthy dynamic for the sales leader and the marketing leader to be at odds.

They should work in unison.

Where is the technology going? What is the competition doing? What do your customers say about your pricing, your product, your features, your service?

One way to accomplish this tight, effective communication is through daily "standups." Have the CMO and CSO standup daily with the head of engineering in a quick exchange of thoughts and updates on marketing, sales, and product issues.

The three leaders touch base on progress against goals. They can cover any issues that may have arisen in the last 24 hours, as well as upcoming events. It ensures they are in sync. Whether it's an 8AM coffee or a

5PM beer doesn't matter—meeting daily is extremely helpful. Even if it's through video chat.

All three people should attend and maintain a professional tone. In a two-person meeting, a personality clash could result in a "he said/she said" as to what transpired.

The dynamic of the sales and marketing organizations and their work together, is a delicate dance which can be beautiful, or it can be disastrous. If the two leaders can't dance together, there's no party.

The Sales/Marketing Dance

Sales and marketing need each other to be complete and effective. These two disciplines are reliant on one another for a successful outcome. When both succeed, the company wins. When there's blame and finger-pointing, everybody loses.

However, these two disciplines must remain somewhat independent to be healthy and productive. The current trend is toward appointing a Chief Revenue Officer (CRO) who takes responsibility for both sales and marketing.

If you structure your organization this way—combining these two roles into one position—ensure that both roles get equal attention and weight.

Whenever I've seen this structure, the dual role usually goes to someone with a sales background and limited marketing experience, and things get lopsided. This can lead to decisions being made from a sales perspective and not a holistic or balanced perspective.

A better way to set this up is to have a VP/Director of Marketing and their counterpart from Sales reporting in to the CRO.

Sales sometimes sees marketing as less urgent, because marketing often takes a long-term view. Sales is often focused on short-term revenue to meet quarterly and annual quotas. Marketing has a dual role to play. We must focus on the current promotions and programs that support the sales team in meeting quarterly quotas. *And*, we must also monitor the future of the company—looking at revenue and product mix for the current year and further down the road.

We can also view marketing as less important than sales because the big-picture goal is generating sales and paving the path to revenue. Enabling the sale is just as important as closing the deal. You can't have one without the other. If both groups are working together in alignment, they can merge into one healthy revenue growth picture.

Get On The Same Page

Marketing and sales work on a spectrum of activities together to drive results, including the website, collateral, promotions, e-mail campaigns, events, and many others. Here are three projects that are especially important for sales and marketing to undertake *together,* in alignment.

1. Agree on the unique value proposition and the messaging.

It's marketing's job to articulate the unique value proposition, capture it in writing in an elevator pitch, and make sure that it's as compelling as it can possibly be.

We need to hear the sales team say "*YES, that's it!*"

If, on the other hand, the sales team has not "bought into" the value proposition and messaging, they won't use it.

Each sales director, rep or channel partner will have their own pitch deck with their own thoughts and words. What's wrong with that, you ask? The company is losing out on the synergy of consistent messaging. If everyone in the company is using the same words to describe the same benefits, in the same order of importance, it becomes like a mantra. If all employees can recite key messages, whether in front of a customer or over beer with friends, it maximizes the benefit of that continuity.

That job is not really "done" until that messaging resonates with the target customer. With your customers' blessing on the messaging, it will translate into revenue. *That* is the real market validation of your offering and the way you've communicated it.

And *that* serves the company well.

2. Agree on the target customer.

The people most likely to buy your products or services share some common characteristics, like demographics, job roles, responsibilities, and behaviors.

The more clearly you define your target group, the more you understand where and how to reach your best prospects. A buyer persona is a model that describes your typical or target customer, based on detailed audience research. Ensure that sales and marketing agree that this is your target customer.

There's often a tendency to resist nailing this down and keeping the target broad to avoid ruling out any prospective buyers.

Don't be tempted to do this. It often results in watered down messaging that makes your offering less compelling in the eyes of the audience you want to reach.

3. Develop lead qualification criteria.

Sales and marketing leaders should develop lead qualification criteria *together*. As you develop the criteria, take time to agree on terminology.

Work together to define what you will call a "lead," a "prospect," a "suspect," and an "opportunity." That will help get everyone on both teams onto the same page. Have consistent definitions for each of these terms so you are both using the same vocabulary to mean the same thing.

There are many terms used in lead management that vary from company to company. Inside your own firm, though, it will serve you well to have sales and marketing teams using the same definitions.

Example:

- 10,000 people attend a network security trade show. My company makes network security solutions, so the 10,000 show visitors are my "**suspects**."

- 2,000 of those stop by my booth and agree to have their badge scanned. These are my "**prospects.**"
- 400 of those had a conversation with someone on my team. Those are my "**leads.**" We will divide these into qualified/unqualified leads based on our pre-defined criteria. Do they have a defined initiative? Do they have budget? Do they have purchase responsibility? Do they have purchase authority? Do they have a purchase timeframe in mind?

MARKETING FUNNEL

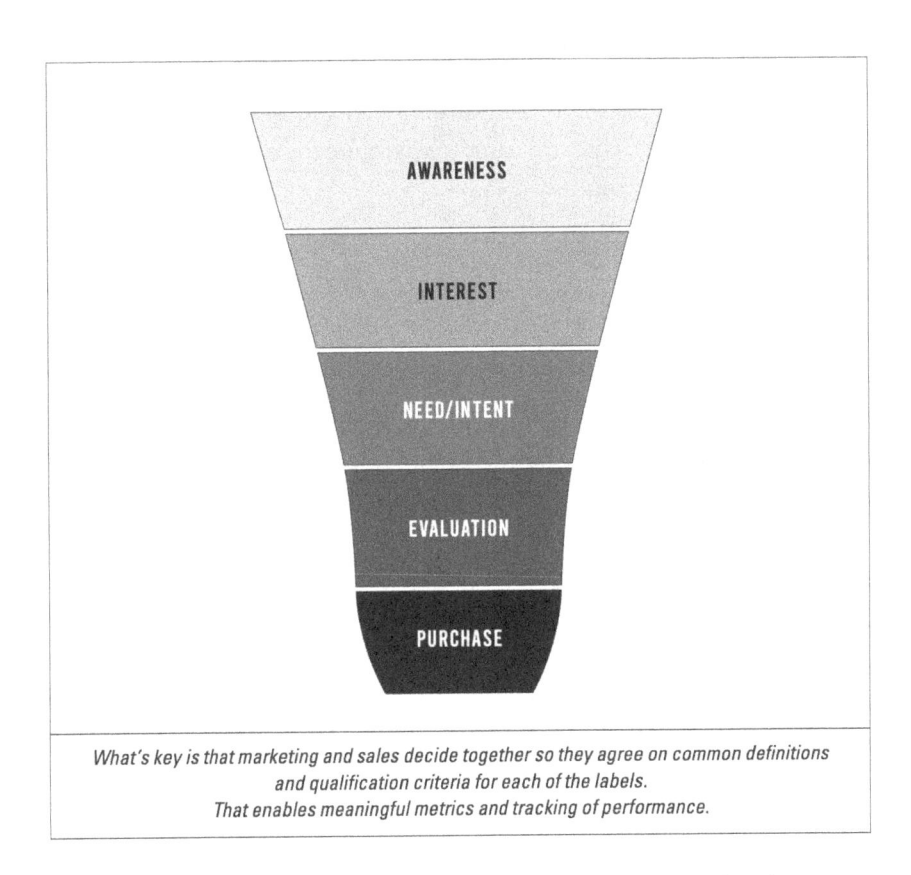

AWARENESS

INTEREST

NEED/INTENT

EVALUATION

PURCHASE

What's key is that marketing and sales decide together so they agree on common definitions and qualification criteria for each of the labels.
That enables meaningful metrics and tracking of performance.

- 35 of those 400 are actual "**opportunities**" because they have an initiative and a budget for it, plus the buying responsibility and authority to purchase.

The numbers are not important, nor are the labels. (I've seen sales funnels with the top labeled "suspects" or "prospects" or "leads." Whatever.) Just be consistent. What's key is that marketing and sales decide together so they agree on common definitions and qualification criteria for each of the labels.

This example is a trade show scenario. These leads were captured in person from visitors to a trade show booth. The same exercise can be done online, with your website visitors. Develop appropriate qualification criteria, such as time spent on the site, videos viewed, whitepapers downloaded, information supplied, etc.

4. Report on status/progress using joint metrics

When we have terms *and* transitions defined and agreed upon between marketing and sales, then we can use that nomenclature to communicate and report on progress.

Jointly defining this makes it hard to argue with a report that shows four hundred leads and thirty-five opportunities in the pipeline. A data-driven organization from top to bottom provides meaningful information.

Unfortunately, mismatch is common! According to a recent Gartner webinar, *Top CSO Priorities for 2020*, chief sales officers came up with three areas of focus for top sales executives:

- Sales manager effectiveness
- Prospecting and early pipeline activities
- Account growth[2]

Digging into the second area,, Gartner stated that "Sales teams reject 55 percent of marketing-qualified leads (MQLs)."[3] That underscores the need to agree on qualification criteria. If you ensure that everyone on both teams understands and agrees with the qualification criteria, it will eliminate most of the gray area.

And prevent a lot of gray hair as well.

The Importance of Aligning Sales and Marketing

Alignment between sales and marketing is crucial to the success of the marketing team, the sales team and ultimately, the company itself. Develop a way to share information and to build a feedback loop into your internal processes. Marketing managers, directors, and VPs can go on sales calls. Arrange on- and off-site meetings with the two departments to get in sync on all related topics, both large and small.

The marketing team needs sales help to get customer feedback on many product issues, including product positioning, service, pricing, and future product needs. Sales needs marketing's help to have the most effective sales tools always at the ready.

> *"When sales and marketing align, your company optimizes their marketing and sales cycles as a whole, resulting in reduced costs and an increase in growth. Sales and marketing alignment can lead to a 32 percent increase in year-over-year (YoY) revenue growth."*[4] —Aberdeen Group, "Why Alignment Is Worth The Effort" Feb. 2016

We've all heard evidence of misalignment between sales and marketing. If you hear your sales director saying, "The leads we got from marketing are no good!" while your marketing director complains, "Sales isn't following up to close on these leads!" Consider that a red flag. Time and money are being wasted.

If that's happening in your organization, there's a good chance that both the processes and the relationship may need some attention.

And it will be well worth it.

APPLICATION

To align marketing and sales, here are some steps that can resolve the issue and get sales and marketing on track.

1. Agree on the unique value proposition and messaging.

2. Agree on the definition of your target customer. Resist the temptation to keep the target broad to include all possible prospective buyers. Don't do that. Instead, do the work to nail it down.

3. Develop lead qualification criteria *together*.

4. Conduct regular pipeline reviews with the lead criteria in mind.

5. Agree on a dashboard that reports on progress against goals, using joint metrics that have been agreed upon by both marketing and sales.

6. Assess the effectiveness of marketing campaigns by tracing progress back to the lead source, whatever it may be (e.g., marketing campaign, trade show, sales rep, etc.).

7. Meet weekly to review and report on status. Discuss, tweak, repeat.

8. Strive for full transparency. It's the only way you can assess progress, identify obstacles, and improve both processes.

9. Watch to ensure that the two function heads work well together and respect each other. This will best serve the company.

FINAL THOUGHTS

Transparency is critical. It allows us all to know how we are doing and what needs improvement. It also allows us to measure our progress and report on current status. A focus on lead transparency can increase trust in the sales / marketing partnership. The more these two organizations work together, collaborate, and stay in sync, the more the company benefits.

During and after the lead qualification process, make it very clear who does what. Be very clear on the recommended follow-up actions for each prospect or lead.

Sales and marketing alignment directly affects the bottom line of the organization. Therefore, it's well worth the effort. A key indicator of misalignment is finger-pointing, while a key indicator of alignment is transparency.

Both teams have the information needed to improve the efficiency of the buyer's journey from awareness to purchase. It's important that sales and marketing work together and have a healthy, open, respectful relationship with frequent ongoing communication.

That openness will enable them to adapt both sales and marketing strategies as demanded by the market, the customer, and the competition to maximize and speed up growth. When sales and marketing work together, the organization has a greater chance of sustained success.

Sales and marketing alignment also helps keep the focus on the customer. Therefore, it's a key factor in ensuring long-term viability for the company. Stay on the *Path to Revenue* and be that one in ten that remains successful and sustains growth.

Just as your teams must work together, the steps in a marketing process must, too.

The same is true if you build your marketing plan out-of-sequence, as I will show you in Chapter 10.

10

DEFINING YOUR MARKET STRATEGY

You may wonder why the topic of strategy is covered toward the end of the book. At a glance, it could seem like a logical starting place.

But it isn't.

Marketing strategy formulation, done well, requires that the results of your vast intelligence gathering—on customers, on the market, on competitors—are put through a rigorous, customer-centric analysis. That research, plus thoughtful analysis, must be conducted prior to developing your marketing strategy.

In short, ensure that you know your customer and your market well before embarking on your go-to-market journey.

A Few Definitions

This book is intended to help smaller companies and technology startups. Often the first product or service these organizations launch also launches the company. That first product or service is the whole *reason* the company was created. That said, it may be helpful to take a big-picture view of the difference between marketing strategy and go-to-market strategy.

- A **marketing strategy** enables your company to reach the target **market** they've identified and deliver on its value proposition over time. It's a long-term, big picture concept.
- A **go-to-market strategy** enables your company to bring products and services to market. It's a short-term initiative driven by a specific new product or service.

Marketing and go-to-market strategies intersect as you put plans in place to support the overall business objectives of growing revenues and increasing profits. That directly enables the company to return value to shareholders, which is the most fundamental purpose of any business.

This tenet is attributed to Milton Friedman and subscribed to by many leading economists. And this was the consensus in the business world prior to the August 2019 CEO Roundtable in which the purpose of business was "redefined." Now, presumably, the purpose of business is to benefit "all stakeholders–customers, employees, suppliers, communities and shareholders."[1] OK, sure, we'll say businesses exist for 'everyone.' And argue that point some other time. But both definitions agree on one thing: businesses must make a profit to remain viable.

The Use of Market Research

The assumptions upon which your marketing strategy is based can make or break your company. Defining your target customer, understanding customer needs and preferences, knowing how to reach your customers and what motivates them—all of these have ramifications and rewards you'll feel every day for years to come.

The most important phase in the marketing process is understanding your market collectively and really getting to know your customers specifically. We must learn everything we can about our customers. It's that simple.

By definition, when you embark upon a journey to learn something, you don't already know everything about that subject. Start with that. We don't know, but we want to learn.

When you have this mindset, astonishing things can occur.

The customer might tell you what they *really* need—maybe something with much greater potential than what you had planned to make. Done properly, learning a market is not a matter of boring statistics—it's a vital, exciting interaction with customers and industry resources.

While consumer products are often market-researched to death, technology products tend to be insufficiently studied.[2]

The discipline we put in place in consumer-packaged goods does not seem to have carried over into the world of technology. Even with B2B products and services, I cannot overstate the importance of knowing your customer. Make assumptions carefully. Educated guesses must be very well-informed, but it's still important to test theories to prove or disprove hypothetical arguments.

When devising your market research efforts, a combination of all available approaches will serve you best. Talking and listening. In-person discussion and written questionnaires. Ask and observe. Include everyone involved in the buying process. Remove all the limitations you can and consider all the input you can get. As mentioned at the beginning of the book, market research is most helpful and reliable to *improve* your product or service, rather than to dictate what you *should be* creating. It is nearly impossible to get accurate commentary on something that hasn't been created yet.

Current, Traditional Thinking

Develop your go-to-market strategies by thinking through the "Who, What, When, Where, Why" questions. Most books and articles you'll read on this will state them like this:

- *Who* I sell to
- *What* I sell
- *When* I sell
- *Where* I sell
- *Why* I sell
- *How* I sell my product or service to that customer

Market research with this thinking might start with the premise that my company plans to sell either Product A or Product B. Questions might include:

- Which do you prefer, Product A or Product B?
- Why do you prefer B?
- Where would you expect to buy B?
- Are there any other features you need added to Product B?
- In its current state, how much would you be willing to pay for Product B?
- If we added the features you're suggesting, *then* how much would you be willing to pay for Product B?

From there, you would typically develop your product strategy, as well as your communications strategy, channel selection, and pricing.

This book is about *challenging you to re-think your entire approach* with a customer-centric mindset. In starting with your offer, you're asking about the market for a solution you've already designed in your mind and plan to sell.

Rather than starting with your offer, you start with the customer.

Customer-Centric Thinking

What is the customer doing—feeling/thinking/frustrated with/trying—that prompts the need to buy something for that purpose?

What can we learn about that need? What's the situation before you came along? Now, with that in mind, let's go back to thinking through the Who, What, When, Where, Why & How questions.

Ask those questions with a *customer-centric mindset*. With the customer in mind, develop your product strategy, communications strategy, channel selection, and pricing. Here are some leading questions that will help you to answer from the customer viewpoint.

CUSTOMER-CENTRIC APPROACH TO MARKET STRATEGY

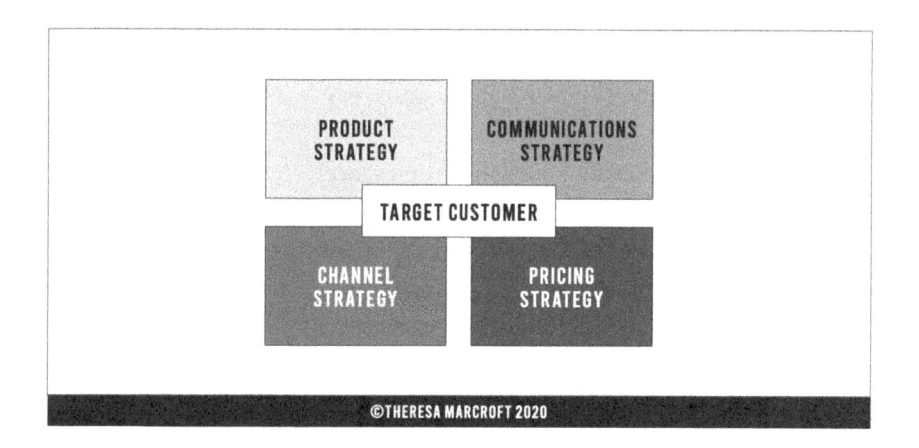

[Diagram: Four quadrants labeled PRODUCT STRATEGY, COMMUNICATIONS STRATEGY, CHANNEL STRATEGY, PRICING STRATEGY surrounding a central TARGET CUSTOMER box. ©THERESA MARCROFT 2020]

Product Strategy: Questions to Keep in Mind

- What is the (unmet) need my customer wants to satisfy?
- What is causing their pain desire/hunger/ etc.?
- What's the trigger that might spark their interest in my offering?
- How will they likely use my product or service?
- What are the "must haves" and the "nice to haves"? (features and benefits)
- What products or services does my customer consider to be alternative solutions? (competition)
- Would those competitive solutions more effectively meet their needs? If not, what would?

All the above questions go into your customer-centric approach to product strategy.

THERESA MARCROFT

Communications Strategy: Questions to Keep in Mind

- How will I present my offering to the market so it resonates with my customer? What messages will they find most interesting and meaningful?
- How will my customer find me? Will I reach them best on social media? If so which channels should we use?
- Which traditional press does my customer consume (news outlets, magazines, online publications, white papers, reviewers (like C|NET)?
- How will my customer view other comparable solutions/companies/products and services? What else will they customer consider to be competitive solutions to meet this same need? (positioning)
- What will my customer consider to be the differences between those offerings and mine? (differentiation)?
- How does my customer prioritize needs?

All the above questions go into your customer-centric communications strategy.

Channel Strategy: Questions to Keep in Mind

How will the customer prefer to buy my product or access my service:

- From a big store? A systems integrator? An independent consultant?
- Does my customer want to buy online?
- Does my customer need to trust the seller for advice and input?
- Does my customer need to rely on the seller's technical expertise?
- How will I assure my customer of the needed level of after-sales service?

All the above questions go into your customer-centric channel strategy.

Pricing Strategy / Questions to Keep in Mind

- Does my customer value top quality and expect to pay a higher price for it? or,
- Does my customer most appreciate a low price?
- Is the market pricing a cost-plus profit model? Or is pricing based on an estimate of perceived value?
- Does my customer expect a large variety of add-on options, all priced separately?
- Does the pricing reflect the positioning of the product or service?

All the above questions go into your customer-centric pricing strategy.

Now, Formulate Your Customer-Centric Go-to-Market Strategy.

Now it's time to develop your strategy.

A marketing strategy is like painting your living room. It sounds like a simple task, but there are more steps than you may realize.

Developing a marketing strategy should begin with intimate knowledge of your target profile customer. Add to that a concise review of key market information, including approximate size of the market, estimated growth rate, and relevant market trends.

Follow this synopsis with strategic recommendations. Comprise the core marketing strategy of the four sections in the previous graph. Draft an outline of your marketing plan. Base this outline on your answers to the questions in the four sections above.

Always remember that the target customer is at the heart of your endeavor. Answer your Product, Communications, Channel, and Pricing questions by keeping your target customers in mind and asking how they would respond or weigh their options.

Target Customer
Who buys my product?
Who is our target customer profile?
What drives them?
Have we defined our user persona from every angle?
(demographics, interests)
Which vertical markets do we want to target? In what order?

Your market plan begins with your target customer.

Develop your target audience profiles. It's tempting to skip the target audience profile step, *but don't!*

Knowing your target customer will eventually lead you to improved product development, more effective marketing strategies, better positioning, and more compelling communications.

As you develop the profile of your ideal customer, you are segmenting your market and identifying the people you want to target. You are also reviewing the competitive landscape so you can assess which companies are offering other solutions. Maybe they're offering similar solutions; maybe they're offering alternative solutions. Quite possibly, this exercise will reveal potential partners you had not previously considered.

For example, a target customer wants to earn a bachelor's degree. Both brick-and-mortar and online universities may compete for the same person. That same person might also consider a local junior college for two years before transferring to a university to finish that bachelor's.

Different solutions and approaches get the customer to the same end.

Most products and services are not appropriate or attractive to everyone, so you want to define *who* is a suitable target. This will also lead you into thinking about *why* they're a good target. What is it about their need that remains unmet by the competition today?

Now that we understand our customers so well and we have a marketing strategy outlined, we develop our go-to-market strategy.

THE PATH TO REVENUE

Go-To-Market

How we take our product or service to market leverages all the work we just did in marketing strategy development and also adds to the launch plan. You can view it as a new product or service announcement with a *lot* of prep work and a *lot* of follow-up.

The launch plan has these additional components:

- **Market segmentation** plans might include rolling out a new product or service to one vertical market as a learning experience, tweaking the plan based on what you learn, then continuing the rollout to subsequent vertical markets.
- **Sales promotions**, such as introductory pricing or other incentives.
- **Sales training** for all your sales reps and channel partners.
- **Technical training** for your support staff, service rep, and channel partners.
- **Advertising and social media** plans and messaging.
- **Collaboration with partners** who might join in the launch effort. For example, it's my habit to pre-brief international sales partners on upcoming new products so they can localize the announcement in their own country or market. Managing the timing enables a global launch with same-day execution everywhere for greatest impact.
- **Distribution plans** to get the product to the customer—whether through online sales and physical shipment, downloading of software, or some combination.
- **Customer training** on this specific new product or service.
- **Training program** for post-sales support and service personnel
- **Launch program** tactics.
- **Launch budgets** for both marketing and sales.

Customer-Centric Go-to-Market Numbers Exercise

Marketing is a means to an end.

Think about your current business—what it looks like today—and where you want it to be in two or five years. Your marketing strategy is what will take you there. It's your strategy for getting from point A to point B.

Let's say you want to grow your revenues by 50% over the coming year.

Develop a matrix that breaks down your sources of revenue and compares today and tomorrow.

- Revenue level
- Number of customers
- Revenue by service or product
- Revenue by geographical area
- Revenue by vertical market.
- Revenue by partner or channel.

EXAMPLE: The goal is to grow revenues 50% from $200K to $300K annually.

Tracking your business data, you know how many leads it takes to close one deal. To get from Scenario A (today's $200K revenue level) to Scenario B (next year's $300K revenue goal), you need to add $100,000 to your annual revenue run rate. If your average deal size is $5,000, that means you'll need 20 new customers.

Start by looking at your close rate. Let's say for every deal closed, there were 10 demo appointments. For every demo appointment, there were 40 leads to be qualified. Thus, we need 400 new leads to get one closed deal. Given an average deal size of $5,000, we need 8000 fresh leads to get our additional $100,000 of business next year.

Work backwards to figure out your demand generation targets. Then translate business goals into the number of leads that need to be created to meet the business goals.

THE PATH TO REVENUE

Here's a generic example of how to approach demand generation needed to meet revenue goals:

DEMAND GENERATION EXAMPLE

FOR EVERY 400 LEADS GENERATED		
NUMBER OF QUALIFIED LEADS (1 IN 10)	40	
NUMBER OF DEMO'S CONDUCTED (1 IN 4)	10	
NUMBER OF DEALS CLOSED (1 IN 10)	1	
	CURRENT YEAR	**TARGET GOAL YEAR X**
NUMBER OF CUSTOMERS	40	60
AVERGE DEAL SIZE	$5,000	$5,000
REVENUE	$200,000	$300,000

If the same ratios hold true and we want to increase revenues by $100,000 in Year X, then we need to close 20 new customers @ $5,000 each.

That means we need to conduct 80 demos to get 20 new customers.

To get 80 demos, we need to qualify 800 new leads.

To get 800 qualified leads, we need to generate 8,000 new leads.

And 8,000 new leads generated will add $100,000 in revenue to our business.

Through this exercise, we've explored the "mechanics" of our lead generation and conversion—we've done the math. Now we know what it will take to get the desired increase in revenue. With that insight, we might now determine that our goal isn't feasible. Maybe we change the target to grow 25% annually instead of 50%. Or, we find a way to increase our average deal size or pricing so that meeting the goal won't require so many new customers. Or we find upsell opportunities with existing customers. Whatever the action plan, this insight is vital.

APPLICATION

1. Recognize the value of adopting a customer-centric mindset. Allow it to guide you through all the steps we've discussed.

2. Acknowledge that customer-centric marketing is what gets you from today's revenue level to the level you envision in your three- or five-year plan. Customer-centric marketing enables you to turn your vision for the company into a reality.

3. Swap out traditional thinking. Stop asking, "To whom will I sell?" and "What will I sell them?" Instead, adopt customer-centric thinking, "What does my customer need?" and "What solution are they seeking?"

4. Develop your target audience profiles—the profile of your ideal customer. Know all you can about them.

5. Do the strategic marketing exercises. Keep that customer-centric mindset as you develop the strategies for:

- Your product
- Your communications and positioning
- Your channel
- Your pricing.

6. Marketing strategy is the path that will get you from point A to point B.

Lay out your business objectives for the coming year and do the math to determine your lead conversion rates. Then you'll know the demand generation goals needed to meet your revenue goals and can assess whether they are realistic.

FINAL THOUGHTS

Every time you hear the word "market", think of it as a massive collection of customers. Each customer makes a buy or no-buy decision based on their own needs. That's why the customer-centric mindset is the starting point for your journey on the path to revenue.

The most successful companies are *market-driven*. This is another way of saying that most successful companies are driven by the needs of their customers. This is why the customer-centric mindset is so vitally important.

Collect ample marketing information before you plan strategy. Remember the adage, "Measure twice, cut once." Be sure you have thought through all of these considerations before you commit to a strategy.

Translate your strategy into a series of tactics that will get you there. Write plans and associated budgets for both marketing and sales. The tactical plan dictates the actions and schedules that must be accomplished to meet your goals.

Prepare a budget for each action. Marketing tactics and budgets need to mesh with sales tactics and budgets. This all needs to fit together as complementary parts of the overall initiative, so transparency is helpful.

Refer back to your marketing strategy often and update it as necessary. Marketing is never really completed. Your market is dynamic—always changing as competitors come and go.

Customer needs and wants shift, too.

Every time you win *or lose* a customer, you'll want to understand *why*. Use that information wisely; it might warrant a tweak or two to your marketing strategy. Your marketing strategy should be a living document.

Revenue is always the end goal. The gambling industry creates revenue at an enviable pace. Why? The gaming odds are always in their favor.

The following chapter will highlight things you must do to give your young, growing company the best odds of success.

11

TYING IT ALL TOGETHER: BE THE ONE IN TEN THAT THRIVES!

Launching and growing a successful tech company, maybe becoming the next Apple or Google, sounds exciting, doesn't it?

Often it starts like this.

Someone with great technical skills has an idea for a new product or service. They think about it night and day, sketching their invention around BBQ sauce stains on bar napkins.

When they think they've got it mostly figured out, the founder gathers a core team of people to polish, hone, and tweak the vision. The team starts with the founder's idea and makes it a reality. Once they have a prototype, they hire a sales guy or put up a website to sell it.

Now the core team has grown. The entire company might be twelve or twenty people, tinkering with the product. They're looking forward to *revenue*.

But when you strip away the angel funding, the foosball tables, and the Friday happy hours, what you have left, aside from a bunch of unhappy people, is still just technology.

THERESA MARCROFT

Not a solution.

This core team is in unchartered territory. None of them knows what perils lie ahead, and what challenges await them on the path to revenue.

This company, built on an *idea,* has developed a piece of technology. The team is searching for a market—searching for customers who might have a need for this technology.

As common as this is, it's backwards.

You need to know whom you're serving before you can serve them well.

Not Only For Startups

When I saw this dynamic for the second or third time and was asked to help make the company successful in the long-term, I knew I had to focus my consulting business on this issue. When I saw this dynamic for the tenth time, I knew I had to write a book about it!

The number one reason startups fail—accounting for 42% of failures—is "no market need."[1] No market need means your product has no customers *for the specific combination of features and functionality you're offering.*

The company that sold smart home products to DIY homeowners had an existing market, as evidenced by over a dozen competitive brands of smart home hubs and devices. But the customer, the hands-on DIY buyer, needs ease of use. If you expect them to learn to code, or to somehow demystify complex screens, it just won't fly. Whether your company is a ten-person startup or already at $500 million, this is a costly lesson.

If you define your target customer from the start and do your research, you'll discover what features and functionality will make your offering a success.

If you engineer a very cool piece of technology and then hope to find a market, you've relegated the customer to an afterthought.

THE PATH TO REVENUE

And, if your customer is the afterthought, your company is in trouble.

Getting and Staying on The Path to Revenue

Every company needs to adopt a customer-centric mindset, if they haven't already. This is vital to the development of a go-to-market strategy. Adopting a customer-centric mindset is the culmination of the following strategic projects.

Meet Your Target Customer, Where They Are.

Understanding the technology-adoption life cycle will shed light on various views for adopting new technologies. Read Geoffrey Moore's book, *Crossing the Chasm*. As discussed, some people are early adopters, others are mainstream or late adopters. Some are in between.

Determine what category best fits your product, then understand the mindset of that target market. Doing so is one of the smartest, savviest endeavors you can undertake.

It also guides how you market to that group, based on both what they need to hear and on their attitudes toward new technology. (See Chapter 3).

Use Customer-Centric Messaging to Communicate Value.

Value-based messaging is a rare thing of beauty here in Silicon Valley, where CEOs are usually engineers and tech-speak abounds.

Quoting your product data sheet will not get you anywhere. What benefits does your product deliver to the customer? Figure out how to describe that succinctly, using words that resonate with your customer. Have your 'elevator pitch' always at the ready. (See Chapter 4).

Empower Sales with Customer-Centric Content.

Value to the customer must be well-articulated in your sales materials. Compelling content and effective sales tools are the ammunition that

153

enable your sales team to fight in the market. Arm them well. When your sales team succeeds, everyone wins. (See Chapter 5).

Create And Claim Your Market Niche.

Category creation is a perfectly acceptable and often insightful growth strategy. However, many company leaders can find it intimidating. Sometimes creating and claiming your own market niche is actually the smartest approach. If you can pull it off, you can be king of your own (newly created) market. (See Chapter 6).

Be Savvy About Growing Revenue Channels.

Channel sales, as opposed to direct sales, is a practical approach to getting your company on the path to revenue. Channels are also a vital key to going international. There's a time and place to branch out beyond the US market, and you can be successful with the right research, preparation, timing, and focus. It's not a revenue level or product type that makes you ready. The best advice I can give you is to be certain you've worked out the kinks in your business model here at home first. There are several other areas to consider before building a channel organization and/or moving overseas. (See Chapter 7).

Differentiate Your Offer To Stand Out.

Your differentiation—whether it's brand, product, or experience-based—must be intentional. And strategic. Differentiation is about giving your customer a reason to buy your product or service instead of that of your competitors. This makes your offer rise above or stand out from the dozens of other competitive offerings on the market. Communicate to your target customer that your offering is a better match for their needs than the other available alternatives. (See Chapter 8).

Align Sales and Marketing.

We are partners, not adversaries. Getting your company on the path to revenue requires that marketing and sales work together. Transparency and teamwork are key.

Aligning those two departments not only gives you synergy of message and effort, it also makes each of your processes, programs, and strategies more efficient. (See Chapter 9).

Define your Go-To-Market Strategy.

Going to market has four components; product strategy, positioning & communications, channel strategy, and pricing strategy. Develop all four as a part of your go-to-market initiative, and do so with a customer-centric mindset. (See Chapter 10).

Your company must put a "customer-centric mindset" into your business practice. You can benefit from the eight examples of successful customer-centric initiatives included in this book. They show just how important customer-centric marketing truly is. It makes the difference between business failure and business success.

12

THREE BONUS IDEAS

> Man's mind, once stretched by a new idea, never regains its original dimensions"
>
> —Oliver Wendell Holmes

This book covered eight strategies to build a customer focus into your organization. In addition to those, I want to share three other recommendations. These practical suggestions can have a positive and significant impact on your company's chances for success. One is about being creative in your public relations (PR) efforts, the second is about measuring customer satisfaction, and the third will increase the value you gain from your Board.

Bonus Idea #1: Creative PR Can Be *Very* Powerful

On this path to revenue, consider PR to be the icing on the cake. It doesn't have to be tedious. By taking a new approach, PR can be quite creative.

I'm not talking about designing publicity "stunts" purely to get media attention. That is less appropriate in the B2B world anyway. Creative

PR is brilliantly simple, but also has a message. The PR strategy, like the rest of your marketing, helps the company to attain corporate objectives. Here are a few examples of the creative PR I've leveraged in my career:

Understand what editors want. What are their challenges?
While working with a leading manufacturer of semiconductor capital equipment, I befriended Pete, the editor of a leading semiconductor magazine. I asked him about the headaches of his job. What were his challenges? He shared with me that finding decent cover art for his magazine was his most dreaded task each month.

I told him I could supply cover art whenever he needed it. Artistic equipment shots? No problem! I staged a photo shoot specifically to capture great shots of our equipment with interesting lighting. This resulted in half a dozen magazine covers featuring my client's equipment in stunning photos which highlighted our products. Of course, Pete gave my company the credit for the photo, which was a nice publicity boost.[1]

Make their jobs easier.
When "optical character recognition" was brand new, I launched an OCR product at Comdex, a *huge* consumer technology show. The trade show was infamous for many reasons, but mainly because it was SO large that it was challenging for any company to rise above the noise and get press coverage.

We wanted to showcase our new product at this event. I contacted the *Show Daily*'s media team and offered to donate a free copy of our new software to their press room.

This allowed the journalists covering the show to scan the press releases they wanted to feature in the *Show Daily News*, meaning we did the work for them! No more re-typing press releases (which, coincidentally, is the whole point of OCR software). Each day, they featured the OCR product in a "credit box" on the front page of the *Show Daily*: "Special thanks to...." This led to several interviews for the company

THE PATH TO REVENUE

that was launching the product and an interview for me in a marketing journal.

Appeal to The Masses
Gunshot detection technology is all about sound waves, calculations, algorithms, and GPS coordinates. Turning that into an interesting story about community safety and the security of our children made it suddenly interesting to just about every resident of this country.

The resulting news piece was any marketers' dream coverage: a full two-minute segment[2] on The CBS Evening News. This brought us exposure in hundreds of markets and drew 7.16 million viewers. Others picked up on the news, including the major networks (ABC, NBC, CBS, PBS and Fox TV), major newspapers (*the Washington Post*,[3] *USA Today, the Mercury News, The San Francisco Chronicle*,) online publications (CNET, Bloomberg.com) and vertical publications such as *Campus Safety Magazine*[4] and *Buildings.com*.[5]

With that, we jump-started our demand generation efforts with a wildly successful product launch announcement that made the company a household name. This was the ideal scenario, because then the communities themselves were demanding that their cities adopt this solution. The PR actually generated demand!

Stay open to different angles.
My client wanted to create a new technology category for their website analysis, but there's a limit to the number of publications that want to cover website analysis.

When *Fortune* magazine was scouring the Silicon Valley for great places to work, I contacted the magazine and got their attention with our foosball tables, free Twinkies & Coke, bike rack in the office, and beer bashes on Fridays.

These things were not rare in Silicon Valley, but they were unusual in the editor's eyes. We became known as a super-fun place to work after being featured among *Fortune* magazine's "25 Cool Companies That Make Silicon Valley Go."

Leverage the Technology to Benefit a New User
I mentioned a well-known software filtering company for whom I also did a category creation project, which launched them into the business space. Their legacy product was consumer software that kept kids safe by blocking harmful online content.

Other huge organizations were interested in educating the public about the dangers of the web for children. Some research pointed me to two other opportunities in which we were able to shine:

- McDonalds mentioned us in a flyer about keeping kids safe online. That flyer was distributed to *millions* inside McDonalds' Happy Meals kits.
- The San Jose, California Tech Museum of Innovation (now called simply "The Tech") had its grand opening about the same time. We worked with them on a hands-on educational exhibit that explained content filtering in simple language, in both English and Spanish.

Note how little budget was required for most of these opportunities. It shows the value of thinking outside the box. This is why I call PR the icing on the cake. Go for it! Be creative!

Your team, after recovering from the shock, will thank you.

"Nothing begets creativity like constraints."
–Christopher Mims

Bonus Idea #2: Measure Customer Satisfaction

We've talked a great deal about building a customer focus into your company. Common sense says that *keeping* your customers, and growing your business with each one, is easier than *acquiring* that customer in the first place.

Once you've done the hard work to win over a new customer, of course you want to keep them—so you work to earn their loyalty and expand your business with them.

'Customer retention' refers to your company's ability to keep customers over the long haul. High customer retention is an opportunity to grow revenues; low customer retention means you are most likely losing market share as your customers defect to the competition.

To ensure future revenue growth, *keeping* your customers is not enough. You can leverage your customers' high level of satisfaction to win *more* customers.

How? Through referrals.

Delighted customers will recommend you to others—not because you ask them to, and not because you reward them for their referrals, but because they are *that* pleased with your product or service. Extreme customer satisfaction leads your customers to recommend you. And those honest, spontaneous referrals result in more customers for you.

Now we're talking sustainable growth.

Measure Customer Satisfaction

Anything important is worth measuring.

Customer satisfaction surveys abound. There are many forms, styles and methodologies. One that has gained popularity for its simplicity is the Net Promoter Score (NPS)[6]. Surveys determine which customers are—and are not—"likely to recommend" a company, product, or service to a friend or colleague. On a scale of 0 to 10, "promoters" rate the likelihood of a positive recommendation on the higher end (9 or 10); "detractors" rate the likelihood they'll recommend on the lower end (6 or below). The Net Promoter Score is the difference between them. This is noteworthy because customer recommendations are a direct function of customer satisfaction.

And customer satisfaction can be measured.

Using NPS as an indicator of customer satisfaction and customer loyalty is helpful: not only can you increase your customer base through referrals; you can further increase the business volume with your happy customers through upsell and cross-sell activities. Both become very real growth opportunities when your customers are delighted and customer relationships are strong. Customer satisfaction is a baseline requirement to maximize revenues from existing customers, so it makes good sense to measure it.

NPS, widely adopted by Fortune 500 companies, is used to measure customer satisfaction so that it can be correlated with revenue growth. Many companies conduct these surveys semi-annually to have a metric and track changes in their customer satisfaction scores over regular intervals. Back in Chapter 3, we discussed the importance of having numerous, well-established references to win new customers in the "Early Majority" and "Late Majority" markets. And success in those market segments is required for sustainable growth.

You can contract with any number of professional organizations that will conduct these surveys with you. (Not *for* you, but *with* you.) They'll bring their experience and best practices to your project, design the surveys to get needed feedback in challenging areas, deliver the insight into the areas you've prioritized, and offer detailed recommendations that are both informative and actionable. In this way, you'll get the most value from your customer survey.

One such company I've worked with is Satrix Solutions (https://www.satrixsolutions.com/). (Note the power of an honest, spontaneous recommendation!)

Companies that do undertake an NPS project are rewarded with rich insights and actionable recommendations. The more these are taken to heart and implemented, the greater your ability to improve your offering, differentiate from the competition, strengthen customer relationships and grow your business.

Remember, anything important is worth measuring.

Bonus Idea #3: Corporate Boards Need Marketing Expertise

Boards recruit for the typical roles of audit, compensation, and governance. Yet, as we've discussed, the lack of strategic marketing is at the core of most corporate failures. Most companies have no marketing expertise on their Boards. And, on top of that, they don't even realize that their company is struggling because of market-related issues. Silicon Valley companies, both public and private, could take a fresh approach: add marketing expertise to the Board of Directors.

> *Most companies have no marketing expertise on their Boards. They don't even realize that their company is struggling because of market-related issues.*

It doesn't have to be an additional committee. It could be just one person with expertise in technology marketing who could make a significant impact on the future growth trajectory of the company. Marketing analysis and expertise is a critically needed viewpoint for Silicon Valley companies hoping to win significant market share.

Good marketing is so much more than just social media and events. Excellent marketing strategy, positioning, product launch timing, and a truly customer-centric approach are all critical. Done well, these elements ensure that your company is on track to offer an identified group of target customers a product or service that will be useful to them, at a price they want to pay.

Sometimes, it's just a matter of putting on your customer hat and asking the right questions. Why would someone pay a premium for our solution? What are they using now? What advantage do we have over the closest competitor? How do we test this or that? Why would the customer adopt this new technology? What does the customer need in order to get comfortable with this choice? How do we minimize the perceived risk of adopting new technology?

Customer-centric marketing is your best bet for getting on the path to revenue and being the one in ten that succeeds.

If more companies had marketing experts on their Boards, it's almost guaranteed that the failure rate would decrease. Dramatically.

PARTING THOUGHTS

During the *best* of times, it's not easy to make a young company successful–to apply the technology adoption concepts, simplify messaging, enable sales with great content, create a new market niche, develop efficient channels, differentiate effectively and align sales and marketing. Each of these is a challenging undertaking, but they *are* possible.

You've read in the case-studies here that it is possible to do these things successfully, by investing intentional, focused efforts in research and conversation, along with plenty of trial and error.

Just because nine of every ten technology companies failed in the past, does not mean that pattern must continue. History doesn't have to repeat itself, if we learn from it. Take another look at this chart.[1]

TOP 10 REASONS STARTUPS FAIL

NO MARKET NEED	42%
RAN OUT OF CASH	29%
NOT THE RIGHT TEAM	23%
GET OUTCOMPETED	19%
PRICING/COST ISSUES	18%
POOR PRODUCT	17%
NEED/LACK BUSINESS MODEL	17%
POOR MARKETING	14%
IGNORE CUSTOMERS	14%
PRODUCT MIS-TIMED	13%

RESEARCH BY CB INSIGHTS, 2019 — CBINSIGHTS.COM/RESEARCH/STARTUP-FAILURE-REASONS-TOP

These are the reasons for failure, cited by the 90% who failed.

To help navigate these challenges successfully, hire the most experienced marketing talent you can find to guide you through them. Set yourself up for success with a constant customer-centric mindset.

Adopt that into your own thinking. Teach it to your team. Expect it of everyone in your company.

The success of your company can be your legacy, but so can its failure.

See this as your opportunity to create a great product, or to fill a void in the market. You can create jobs and change lives. Plus, with success comes the ability to be charitable in unparalleled ways. You may create a company that bears your family name and is passed down from one generation to the next. Or you could sell it in a decade to enjoy life. Or start your next business venture.

Any and all of those possibilities are there for you.

Once you've established that there's a market, be bold with your product. Give this life-changing project the best chance to succeed by instilling a customer-centric mindset throughout the organization. Using that mindset in all your business decisions will put your company on the Path to Revenue. Your company *will* be the one in ten that succeeds.

And be the envy of the 90 percent that did not.

THANK YOU!

If you feel this book has helped you on your journey to building a successful sustainable company, please leave a short, honest review on Amazon.com so others can benefit from this knowledge as well.

NOTES

1. 90 Percent of Start-ups Fail: Here's Why

1. *Crossing the Chasm: Marketing and Selling Disruptive Products to Mainstream Customers by Geoffrey A. Moore*
2. Katie Benner, "A Silicon Valley Dream Collapses in Allegations of Fraud," *New York Times* online, 2016.
   https://www.nytimes.com/2016/09/01/technology/a-silicon-valley-dream-collapses-in-allegations-of-fraud.html?_r=0
3. "The Top 20 Reasons Startups Fail," *CB Insights*, online, 2019. https://www.cbinsights.com/research/startup-failure-reasons-top/
4. Ibid.
5. "Potato Parcel Net Worth," *The Wealth Record* online, 2020.
   https://www.thewealthrecord.com/celebs-bio-wiki-salary-earnings-2019-2020-2021-2022-2023-2024-2025/other/potato-parcel-net-worth/
6. https://idgadvertising.com/social-shoutout-bud-light/
7. Susan Berfield, "Domino's Atoned for its Crimes against Pizza and Built a $9 Billion Empire," *BloombergBusinessweek*, March 15, 2017. http://www.bloomberg.com
8. Ibid.

2. The Secret: Being "Customer-Centric"

1. "Our Story," *Trader Joes* website, 2020. https://www.traderjoes.com/our-story
2. Emily Jacobs, "Fifteen States Don't Have Trader Joes," *Daily Meal* online, 2014.
   https://www.thedailymeal.com/15-states-dont-have-trader-joes/21814
3. https://podcasts.apple.com/us/podcast/episode-14-why-is-everyone-so-nice/id1375630453?i=1000438887638
4. https://research.privco.com/trader-joes-and-hermes-high-margins-and-effective-anti-marketing-strategy-c9ff4de53802
5. Rules for Revolutionaries by Guy Kawasaki, © 2000, p. 115
6. "Psychology Behind How Trader Joes Became a Favorite Grocery Store," *CNBC online, 2020*. https://www.cnbc.com/2020/03/09/psychology-behind-how-trader-joes-became-a-favorite-grocery-store.html
7. Deanna Lazzaroni, "75 Quotes to Inspire Marketing Greatness," *Marketing Solutions Blog*, LinkedIn online, 2014. https://business.linkedin.com/marketing-solutions/blog/7/75-quotes-to-inspire-marketing-greatness

NOTES

3. Understanding Your Customers' Mindset

1. Geoff Galat, "5 Steps To Understanding Customer Needs Through Mindset Data," Oracle CX Tech Presentation, October 15, 2018.
2. Throughout the book, all individual names have been changed to protect privacy. Company names are also not mentioned due to confidentiality.
3. https://www.cbsnews.com/news/gunshot-sensing-technology-installed-in-first-u-s-high-school/
4. https://tvbythenumbers.zap2it.com/network-press-releases/cbs-news-original-broadcasts-post-strong-year-to-date-ratings-in-viewers-key-news-demographics/
5. https://www.washingtonpost.com/news/the-switch/wp/2015/09/15/schools-are-looking-to-actual-warzone-technology-to-limit-fatalities-from-the-next-mass-shooting/
6. https://www.campussafetymagazine.com/news/california_school_adopts_gunfire_detection_alert_solution_to_improve_safety/
7. https://www.buildings.com/buzz/buildings-buzz/entryid/301/gunshot-detection-technology-a-new-advantage-in-your-security-arsenal-

4. Communicating Value with Customer-Centric Messaging

1. Rules for Revolutionaries by Guy Kawasaki, © 2000, p 74, Harper Business.

Final Thoughts

1. https://www.jeffbullas.com/

5. Empowering Sales With Customer-Centric Content

1. Blog: 'Content Marketing' by Ryan Floyd, Jan. 2017 https://blog.stormventures.com/content-marketing-6243dbb9e0e2
2. Ryan Erskine, "How to Turn B2B Buyers Into Sales Leads According to Data," *Forbes.com* online, 2017.
   https://www.forbes.com/sites/ryanerskine/2017/12/28/how-to-turn-b2b-buyers-into-sales-leads-according-to-data/#428f73215a18
3. "Hours of Video Uploaded to You-Tube Every Minute," *Statistica.com* online, 2019., https://www.statista.com/statistics/259477/hours-of-video-uploaded-to-youtube-every-minute/
4. David Lumb, "One Billion Hours of You-Tube are Watched Daily," *engadget.com* online, 2017. https://www.engadget.com/2017-02-27-youtube-one-billion-hours-watched-daily.html
5. Erskine, "How to Turn Buyers Into Sales Leads," *Forbes.com* https://www.forbes.com/sites/ryanerskine/2017/12/28/how-to-turn-b2b-buyers-into-sales-leads-according-to-data/#428f73215a18
6. Weinberg and Mares, *Traction*.

NOTES

7. Lori Wizdo, "The Ways and Means of B2B Buyer Journey Maps: We're Going Deep at Forrester's B2B Forum," *Forrest.com* online, 2017.
   https://go.forrester.com/blogs/the-ways-and-means-of-b2b-buyer-journey-maps-were-going-deep-at-forresters-b2b-forum/
8. Erskine. "How to Turn B2B Buyers," *Forbes.com*.
9. "The New B2B Buying Journey," *Gartner.com* online. https://www.gartner.com/en/sales-service/insights/b2b-buying-journey
10. Steven Levey, "Have You Adjusted to these Changes in the B2B Buying Process?" *Forbes Agency Council, Forbes.com* online, 2018. https://www.forbes.com/sites/forbesagencycouncil/2018/05/22/have-you-adjusted-to-these-three-changes-in-the-b2b-buying-process/#131698e8c445
11. https://www.thinkwithgoogle.com/consumer-insights/consumer-trends/the-changing-face-b2b-marketing/
12. Ibid.
13. "Enable Content for Sales," *Vengreso.com* online, 2020. https://vengreso.com/content-for-sales

6. Creating and Claiming your Market

1. http://www.agocg.ac.uk/reports/mmedia/wwwtools/log.htm
2. Rinaldo S. Digorgio, "Monitor Your Web Server in Real Time–Part 1," *InfoWorld* online, 1996 https://www.javaworld.com/article/2077130/monitor-your-web-server-in-real-time--part-1.html)
3. Eddie Yoon and Linda Deakon, "Why It Pays to Be a Category Creator," *Harvard Business Review,* 2013. https://hbr.org/2013/03/why-it-pays-to-be-a-category-creator
4. Statista Research Department, statista.com online, Aug. 1, 2018.
5. Keith Naughton, "Cyberslacking," *Newsweek* online, 1999. https://www.newsweek.com/cyberslacking-164428
6. Ibid.

Final Thoughts

1. Eddie Yoon, "Why Category Creation is the Ultimate Growth Strategy," *Harvard Business Review,* 2011. https://hbr.org/2011/09/why-category-creation-is-the-u
2. "MySpace," *Wikipedia* online, https://en.wikipedia.org/wiki/Myspace

7. Being Savvy about Channel Growth

1. Marcus Cauchi, "Podcast: The Inquisitor–with guest Nick Jones," October 17, 2019. https://marcuscauchi.podbean.com
2. "Channel Partner Programs," *CXL.com* online, https://cxl.com/blog/channel-partner-programs/

NOTES

8. Differentiate to Stand Out

1. *https://corporatefinanceinstitute.com/resources/knowledge/strategy/product-differentiation/*
2. "What is Product Differentiation," Corporate Finance Institute online, https://corporatefinanceinstitute.com/resources/knowledge/strategy/product-differentiation/
3. https://www.redestelecom.es/gestion/entrevistas/1065287001403/lucierna-abraham-nevado-cto.1.html, 2013.
4. "Product Differentiation is Important in Today's Financial Climate," *Investopedia* online, 2018.
   https://www.investopedia.com/ask/answers/062415/why-product-differentiation-important-todays-financial-climate.asp
5. "Product Differentiation," *Corporate Finance Institute* website, https://corporatefinanceinstitute.com/resources/knowledge/strategy/product-differentiation/

Final Thoughts

1. Ibid.

9. Aligning Sales and Marketing

1. Aberdeen Group, *"Why Alignment Is Worth The Effort,"* Feb. 2016. https://www.aberdeen.com/cmo-essentials/marketing-and-sales-two-positions-one-team/
2. Gartner webinar, "Top CSO Priorities for 2020," 2020.
3. Ibid.
4. Aberdeen Group, *"Why Alignment Is Worth The Effort,"* Feb. 2016.

10. Defining Your Market Strategy

1. "Business Roundtable Redefines the Purpose of a Corporation to Promote 'An Economy That Serves All Americans,'" *Business Roundtable* online, August 2019.
   https://www.businessroundtable.org/business-roundtable-redefines-the-purpose-of-a-corporation-to-promote-an-economy-that-serves-all-americans
2. Paul, Sherlock, ReThinking Business to Business Marketing, (The Free Press, 1991). With very special thanks to my friend, the late Paul Sherlock.

11. Tying it All Together: Be The One in Ten that Thrives!

1. "The Top 20 Reasons Startups Fail," *CB Insights*, online, 2019. https://www.cbinsights.com/research/startup-failure-reasons-top/

NOTES

12. Three Bonus Ideas

1. https://wikivisually.com/wiki/Semiconductor_International
2. https://www.cbsnews.com/news/gunshot-sensing-technology-installed-in-first-u-s-high-school/
3. https://www.washingtonpost.com/news/the-switch/wp/2015/09/15/schools-are-looking-to-actual-warzone-technology-to-limit-fatalities-from-the-next-mass-shooting/
4. "California School Adopts Gunfire Direction Alert Solution to Improve Safety," *Campus Safety Magazine online, June 2015.* https://www.campussafetymagazine.com/news/california_school_adopts_gunfire_detection_alert_solution_to_improve_safety/
5. Theresa Marcroft, "Gunshot Detection Technology: A New Advantage In Your Security Arsenal," *Building.Com* online, 2016.
   https://www.buildings.com/buzz/buildings-buzz/entryid/301/gunshot-detection-technology-a-new-advantage-in-your-security-arsenal-
6. Net Promoter, Net Promoter Score, and NPS are trademarks of Satmetrix Systems, Inc., Bain & Company, Inc., and Fred Reichheld.

Parting Thoughts

1. Graph reprinted with permission from CBInsights.
   https://www.cbinsights.com/research/startup-failure-reasons-top/

ABOUT THE AUTHOR

Theresa Marcroft has spent two decades helping technology company CEOs succeed. In 2017, the Silicon Valley Business Journal named her a *Silicon Valley Woman of Influence*.

Through her marketing agency, MarketSavvy, she has advised public and private company CEOs on marketing strategy and implementation. Her consulting work has contributed to twelve successful exits: three IPOs, five successful acquisitions and four companies on the path to sustainable revenues that today total over $10 billion in annual sales.

Theresa has an innate ability to help companies diagnose potential issues then correct their course. She has launched companies, established and built brands, positioned new products and services, taken numerous companies to market, and significantly grown revenues and market share.

Theresa is an expert in marketing disruptive technologies and applying "technology adoption life cycle" concepts. Her prowess with positioning, messaging and market strategy is well known in Silicon Valley's tech industry. Theresa has the people-skills, savvy and upbeat personality to build and lead highly effective teams in emerging market companies. Theresa's career took root at Regis McKenna Inc., the well-respected pioneer of tech marketing, where she worked directly with Geoffrey Moore, author of *Crossing the Chasm*. She has focused her marketing career mainly on enterprise software/SaaS and network security companies.

Theresa earned a B.S. in Marketing from Santa Clara University and a master's degree *magna cum laude* in International Management from the prestigious Thunderbird School of Global Management—the institution voted the '*#1 International MBA Program in the World*' for fourteen consecutive years by *US News & World Report*.

After earning her master's degree, Theresa had a truly global marketing career. She has done business in over 30 countries, including living and working in Austria for four years. She has lead marketing for her clients across Europe, Asia Pacific, and Latin America.

At this writing, she serves on the corporate Boards of two non-profit organizations, Unplanned Good (http://unplannedgood.org) and Pharaoh's Daughters (https://pharaohsdaughters.com/). Theresa also served for four years on the Board of Westminster Woods Camp and Conference Center (https://www.westminsterwoods.org/).

To discuss Board roles, speaking, or strategic marketing consulting, contact Theresa directly at tmarcroft@market-savvy.com. Get more information at https://www.market-savvy.com/speaking.

ACKNOWLEDGMENTS

With warm appreciation of my clients over the last two decades; for all the growing and learning we did together. I'm thrilled for you and your success.

With special thanks to Janet Marcroft and Patricia Watkins for their insightful feedback on each and every chapter throughout the writing process.

Many thanks also to Heidi Bogert, Catherine Marcroft, Maria Z Middleton, Kelly Perey, Sherry Prescott-Willis and Amy Rabinovitz for their astute comments and suggestions.

I'm grateful to you.